WHY ARE YOU NOT SUCCESSFUL NOW?

10 Steps to Get Ahead

By: Baje Fletcher

GOAL GROUP PUBLISHING
Edited by: Michael S. Nixon

THE
GOAL GROUP

PRINTED IN THE UNITED STATES OF AMERICA

Visit the website: www.TheGoalGroupinc.com for more information on products, projects or the author.

Cover designed by: Ques Williams of Midas Touch Creative Group.com

ISBN# 978-1537416885

This book is dedicated to my mentors:

James Cannon & Annetta Bryant.

*"Thank you for seeing greatness in me ...
and pushing me until I saw it in myself."*

Table of Contents

Acknowledgements

First of all, I want to thank God who has pulled me through so many situations that could have broken me down, some of which my closest friends know nothing about. Secondly, to my grandmother Syble Dixon, I want to thank you for instilling strength in me. As a teen I could not understand your way of doing things but now as a woman I realize that you only tried to protect me and steer me in the right direction. Your tough love made me a self-sufficient woman. I spent more time with you than I did with my own parents; you are and will always be my backbone. Since I began writing this book you passed on but you will never be forgotten. You are cherished.

To my parents, life doesn't always go according to plan but I know that you both did your best. Daddy, I was such a rebellious teen, it's amazing how forgiving you are. Now that I'm a woman with responsibilities of my own, I learned to truly appreciate the sacrifices you made. I love you. Mom, you're no longer here physically, but I know you're here in spirit. I will never meet another woman so ladylike and so humble. You are deeply missed, but I know you're in a better place.

Forward

Baje Fletcher has learned how to speak up and ask, even demand what she wants out of life. And she uses her voice and her pen to do just that. In her third book, "Why Are You Not Successful Now? - 10 Steps to Get Ahead", Baje poses a very poignant question that many of us ask everyday. She questions the reader not in the way of judging, but in the way that a person sincerely and compassionately asks another, why are you suffering? Or why are you not doing the things you want. Because from Baje's perspective, you should be successful and do the things you want everyday. It is her earnest desire that everyone who wants to be successful is successful, and she intends to help with that. In the book, Baje gives us 10 steps and an innumerable number of strategies and tips to help us answer the question.

In this book she candidly shares her life's stories and personal secrets for the sake of helping others face their fears, move past their inhibitions and embrace success. Her rags to riches tale begins with a challenged childhood that included divorced parents, living in an impoverished country, foster homes, cold showers, family tragedy, physical and emotional pain. And as she matured in age, people would try and marginalize her in the modeling industry, which is filled with naysayers and evildoers. Baje used all of this adversity, pain and the naysayers to be the catalyst to fuel and fire up her future. Her humble and at times hungry beginnings have given her an insatiable appetite for success. All of which she shares in her book.

When I first met Baje Fletcher several years ago, I was intrigued by her life's story. Coming from such humble beginnings in New York and Jamaica, then going on to become a successful model, entrepreneur, author and a great mother, is not common. Nor is it common for a person to remain so centered and grounded in who they are as they become more and more successful. I recall one story when Baje was talking about her early years in the modeling and entertainment industry. Many of her female peers were doing promiscuous and even unscrupulous things for the sake of fortune and fame. But Baje was having none of that. She was determined to be successful on her terms and no one else's.

While many of her colleagues where thinking of how much money they could make and the success that they could garner by compromising themselves, Baje's thoughts were centered on how much of herself she would lose by doing so. And what type of example would she set for her daughter and the other young women who undoubtedly looked up to her.

Her moral compass and the positive, loving yet stern words of her Jamaican grandmother, held true and ever-present in here mind. So she chose to temporarily abandon this successful career that she had built in modeling and entertainment in order to move towards pursuing her true purpose. That purpose is to help and aid others in finding their purpose and living the lives that they were intended to lead. So she started her company the GOAL Group, which as the name implies, all about helping people set, meet and surpass their life's goals. Since its inception, the GOAL Group has inspired and mentored thousands of people through tutorials, workshops and publications.

Whether your goal is to have financial freedom, start a non-profit, travel around the world, create wealth for your family, go to college, live debt-free or start your own business, Baje and her teachings can help you achieve your goals.

Overcoming so much so early and so often as a young-woman should serve as inspiration for young women around the world. Baje is an example of how you can have it all. She is a loving mother, an author, a successful entrepreneur, a beautiful model, a dedicated sister to her special needs siblings, world traveler, and founder of a community-based non-profit.

She has traveled to more than 12 countries seeking to expand her knowledge and prove that how low you start in life has nothing to do with how high you can soar, literally. Private jet setter in one instance and handing home-cooked meals to homeless people on a Sunday, Baje has a wide perspective on people and life. This has afforded her the unique ability to learn, absorb, refine and share the lessons that she has learned from the countless number of people that she calls mentors and role models.

This book delivers priceless lessons in an unadulterated style. This gained from years of life's experiences and realizing that tough love, is often the best love when it comes to helping others overcome challenges, find their purpose and pursue their dreams. As you read this book you will find aspects of yourself in many of the chapters and lessons. With key themes like guard your vision, change your environment, and ask for what you want, Baje challenges us to take control over our lives and our destinies.

The real power in anyone reaching their goals...is that they inspire others to do the same.

- Kevin R. McGee. Business Coach & Founder and CEO of Avid Entrepreneurship, a social enterprise consultancy founded to help first generation entrepreneurs build better businesses.

speaktome@kevinRmcgee.com   www.kevinRmcgee.com

Introduction

If only I discovered the lessons I know now even five years sooner...I'd be a lot further in life. I wish there was **one** book that introduced me to the law of attraction, taught me about managing my finances, managing my time, setting goals, letting go of dysfunction, and collaborating with others...all in one. I had to find out about all these different aspects of success through different methods and various books. For you on the other hand, this is a one-stop-shop.

I summed up most of what I know about being successful in this book. Some of these lessons I've learned from trial and error, some from books, workshops, webinars, seminars and tutorials. Most from mentors that I've met along the way (some of which I only had the pleasure of speaking to once, and some who have been in my life for years and still are today). The most important thing that I've learned about being successful is that it always begins with one thing...a clear vision. Once you can visualize where you want to be, then you are already half way there.

Along your journey the road to success will sometimes seem lonely. It may require you to change or eliminate your current circle of friends if they aren't on the same wavelength, or if they aren't trying to move into the direction you're moving in. Keeping this book to revert to will come in handy when you need direction, strength or just validation. I'll provide lessons I uncovered, motivational quotes that kept me inspired and real life stories that I learned a tremendous amount from and I'm sure you will as well. Enjoy!

Chapter 1

Envision Success

ENVISION SUCCESS

LESSON 1: No one ever became successful on accident.

Success starts with a vision! I challenge you to redefine success for yourself. Though success is what all of us strive for, success varies widely to each person. To some, to live comfortably and be able to afford everything that they *need* defines success. While to others, success means to be abundantly wealthy and be able to afford everything that they *want* for themselves, family *and* friends.

What does success mean to you?

_____

_____

_____

_____

There is no one precise way to achieve success. There are many roads that lead to this place we so covertly crave. But one thing for sure is: no one has ever become successful without first having a *clear* vision, then a plan to materialize that vision and finally executing that plan.

You can get a vision while you're asleep as a dream, you can get one while daydreaming wide-awake. Perhaps it comes to you in a flash or someone paints a vivid picture in your mind by something great that they accomplished or even by something that they casually implied. Vision is what molds our world. The television programs that we watch, the cars we drive, the beds we sleep in, and the houses that we live in, all started out as somebody's vision. Those visions took on a life of their own when the creation process was started. Some visions are as small as a paper clip or toothpick and some grow as large as stadiums or skyscrapers. Some visions are dormant inventions and some are potential accomplishments.

When you do get a vision it's up to you to keep it vibrant. You have to come up with ways to keep that picture vivid on your mind's canvas. If you don't immediately capture your vision with a physical depiction, like jotting down your vision on paper, intricate details of it can be easily forgotten...forever.

LESSON 2: There is "magic" in words, that's why it's called "spelling".

THE ART OF VISUALIZING

The key is to paint a picture so clear that you actually feel like you're there. What does success feel like? What does fine dining taste like? What does your dream house look like? What does peace of mind sound like? What does the interior of your new car smell like? Visualize the life that you want and everything that you want to accomplish. Visualize everything that you want to have, where you want to live, your dream career, your dream mate, your dream kids, your dream bank account. Take a moment to close your eyes...*right now*...and visualize your dream life. Can you see it? Can you see yourself counting all that money? Can you see yourself living in that upscale neighborhood? Can you see yourself at your dream vacation spot? Can you see your kids in a private school? Can you see yourself relaxing out back alongside your crystal blue pool? Can you see yourself getting the respect you deserve from your colleagues? Can you see the world buying your quality products?

LESSON 3: No one becomes successful without first seeing themselves there.

Take a few minutes every single day to close your eyes and see your future the way you want it. At first you may feel silly, or your picture may seem fuzzy, but visualize until your future is as clear as the present. How does it feel? Capture that emotion; Bottle that feeling. Learn to harvest that inspiration so you can reap it in the moments when you need it the most. Don't worry about *believing* it yet, just start by visualizing now. The more you visualize is the closer you'll get to bringing your vision to life.

CREATE A CONSTANT REMINDER

You have to keep that vision in the forefront of your mind. Some people do so by creating a vision board, a goal board, a wish list, or simply by listening to songs that inspire them. I encourage you to come up with creative ways to keep a grasp on your vision. Perhaps making an audio file describing the life you want to create and speaking your vision into the voice recorder on your phone so that you can listen to it regularly.

You don't have to set a lot of time aside to visualize; you can incorporate it in your daily activities, like while you're in bed or while you're exercising. You can even listen to your audio recordings while you sit in traffic or when you have downtime at work.

Find ways to create automatic reminders.
For example:

-Take a photo of something that represents your vision and use it as a screensaver on your computer or use it as the screensaver for your cell phone.

-You can make a photo key chain.

-You can get your inspirational image printed on your favorite coffee mug that you sip coffee out of every morning.

-I've even seen people get small tattoos of things that represent their ultimate dream so they can constantly feel inspired.

-Personally, I keep motivational books on my coffee table, I keep a little sticky note on my laptop and I use bookmarks with motivational quotes.

-I recently created a collage of the people who inspire me and placed a photo of myself amongst all of them.

Create your own unique reminders. There are so many ways you can motivate yourself subconsciously.

LESSON 4: Your subconscious mind is the most powerful tool that will help you to accomplish your goals. (Later on I'll discuss some ways to tap into it).

GUARD YOUR VISION

Guard your vision with your life! Guard it from the naysayers and the dream killers. Like Will Smith said in the movie: *The Pursuit of Happiness*, "People want to tell you that you can't do something because they can't do it. If you have a dream, you have to protect it!" With that said, don't share your dreams with just anyone. The beginning stage of your dream is the most vulnerable stage of your dream. If it's shared with the wrong person and they dismiss your idea or are sarcastic or cynical about it, then they can shut your whole dream down and smash it to pieces even before it begins to take shape.

Keep your vision a secret until you start to make progress. Keep it private until you have started implementing your plans and until you're strong enough to know that you'll keep pushing forward no matter what anyone says.

"People who say your dreams are impossible have already quit on theirs". –Grand Cardone

A GOAL BOARD

A goal board is typically a poster **board** on which you paste or collage images that you've torn out from various magazines. Figuratively speaking, if your vision is the big picture, then physically speaking, your goal board is a series of small pictures that make up the big picture...like a montage.

I made my first goal board when I was around twenty years old. Some of the things I had on it were:
Get my college degree,
Move to Los Angeles,
Get a Mercedes-Benz,
Buy a house,
Learn Spanish,

...And a few other goals. Beside my Goal Board I also taped some of my past bills that were now on my credit report on my bedroom wall, because I finally made up my mind to pay them off. A close "friend" of mine (at the time) saw my goals and told me that they were "far fetched" and that I was taking on too much. He also told me that having all my outstanding debt in plain view was "depressing". He was judging me on *his* capacity but only I knew my potential. So even though his mediocre way of thinking disappointed me, his lack of faith in me didn't deter me. It did the total opposite actually, it fueled me; it fueled me to prove him and anyone else who doubted me wrong.

A few years later I was going through some old photos; in the background of one of the photos I caught a glimpse of something. It was my first goal board mounted on the wall! I had about ten goals listed; Out of all of those ten things, I accomplished nine so far. (The only one left is for me to learn Spanish...I understand bits and pieces, but I still have a goal of becoming fluent). *I thought: Not bad for "far fetched".* Tears of joy slowly filled my eyes and a gradual smile appeared on my face. I was proud of the unwavering individual I became.

With each goal I accomplished, I got a burning desire to tackle even more, so I kept on striving. Seeing my goal board everyday kept me inspired. As for my "friend", from that day, I started to emotionally distance myself for him and anyone else with an "I can't do it" attitude. *Fast-forward years later, not much has changed positively in his life...and I'm not surprised.*

"Most people fail in life not because they aim too high and miss, but because they aim too low and hit"   *– Les Brown*

VISIONLESS

What's even harder for me than seeing someone with a vision struggling to bring it to life...is someone who is just ready to be successful, but doesn't have a clear vision of success. So what should you do if you don't have a clear vision, or a long-term vision at all?

I have a close friend named Ray and as he approached his thirtieth birthday he confided in me. He said that as a young child all he ever wanted to be was *successful*, and he just could not believe that he hadn't found success yet. He was extremely disappointed in himself. He said he's been reading all these self-help books and dedicated himself to taking self-improvement workshops all his life. He said that in all of the books and workshops he learned that he had to have *passion*...and he said that he absolutely does have passion. Once he said that, I got excited for him, because I knew that if he knew what his passion was, I could help him use his passion to generate income. Eagerly I asked him:

"So what are you passionate about Ray?"

He responded,

"I am very passionate about being successful".

I slumped in my chair with disappointment. I asked him if he ever thought about *HOW* he was going to be successful, he said,

"Not in particular, I just know that ever since I was a boy I've had this burning desire to find success and I thought that would be enough".

Well it wasn't. *If you have passion without a plan then you still have a problem.* My heart truly went out to him because he wanted nothing more in life...than to succeed. He just didn't know at what. I tried to break it down for him.

I told him to look at the blank wall in his apartment, and envision the word success at the very top of the wall, then envision himself at the bottom of the wall and ask how was he going to get to success.

LESSON 5: In order to achieve success, you must first define it for yourself.

So yes, for people to be successful they first have to have passion, but they also have to *know* what it is specifically that they're passionate about. It may sounds self-explanatory but there are millions of people who don't know what they're passionate about and as a result they never find success.

"Money is a result of success; money isn't the end result".

LINES OF PASSION

Now I'll advise you do to the same thing that I told Ray to do; Envision success at the top of a wall in your home, better yet...(If you're a visual learner like I am), get a blank piece of paper and write success at the top and your name at the bottom. Now draw a line from your name to success. The line represents the method that you are going to use to become successful. Along that line write one thing that you're passionate about. You may have more than one thing that you're very passionate about. If so, draw one line for each of those things. The amount of lines per person may vary because there are many roads to success and some people may be passionate about more things than others. However, keep in mind that the more passion lines (or options) you have to success, may result in more distractions as well. Each passion requires time, finances and energy from the next. So only list things that you can see yourself doing for the rest of your life. Now break each line into twelve months, and for each month, list at least one thing that you want to accomplish that month.

Let's use five *Lines of Passion*. Yes five is a lot but it's better to start with too much than too little. (You can narrow them down in the next few days and weeks). After you've narrowed down five things that you're passionate about (or five things that would make you happy); then at the top of each Line of Passion, list five ways you can actually make money doing each of those things. Go ahead and get a pen and start now.

LESSON 6: It's impossible to be successful doing something that you don't love.

If you are one of the people who know you want to be successful but you don't know what it is that you want to be successful at, ask yourself this. If you had all the money that you wanted, what would you do each day? Would you still work in the field that you're in? If not, then what field would you go into? Would you spend your time volunteering? Would you travel internationally? Would you spend more time partaking in your favorite hobby? If so, find a way to do that particular thing full time and figure out a way you can make money doing it. If you love to bake cakes, perhaps you can contact your local bakeries and see if you can drop off some of your signature cakes at the beginning of the week and collect your money and the end of the week. Your sweet delights can be a great addition to their menu if it's something that they don't currently carry or something that they're unable to duplicate. If you have a passion for helping others then you can start a non-profit organization, or you can raise money by putting on fundraisers and collecting donations. If you want to travel the world perhaps you can start a travel group. I'm sure there are people in the world who would love to travel and may even have to money to travel, but don't have anyone to accompany them. For a fee you can put a group together, book the travel, lodging and activities for the entire group and have enough money left over to book your own ticket to travel with them. You have to be creative.

Write down five ways you can make money off of each thing that you're good at. It can be a raw talent, a project, a potential invention or a business idea that you have. For each of those ways you can make money, write down a list of things you would have to do, or implement first before you can start making money. For example: registering your company, building a website, getting business cards made, finding potential clients or buying materials and ingredients to make samples of your product. (Use additional sheets of paper if you have to).

LESSON 7: Follow your passion. Your passion will lead you to success.

JACK OF ALL TRADES

Jack of all trades...but master of none. What if you have too many goals? Sometimes having too many goals is just as bad as having none at all because it's easy to spread yourself too thin. If you aren't able to give your wholehearted attention to any one task in particular then you run the risk of being counterproductive. I do understand that there are some people who are blessed with multiple talents, like Tylor Porry for instance, who wears many hats. He is an actor, producer and director but notice that all three of those talents are in the same field...entertainment. It would have been much harder to capitalize off of three talents, if he was passionate about acting, cooking and fashion designing per se. In the event that you are talented at multiple things that are spread across different industries, then your biggest challenge is going to be narrowing down your focus to the strongest or the one most profitable thing. I'm not saying that you have to put your other dreams on a back burner to die, but you do need to master one thing before you move on to the next. Once you've master your first venture, then things should move more smoothly, because you can use the money coming in from that first venture to funnel into your others.

TALENT IS NOT ENOUGH

Talent alone is never enough. The world is filled with millions of talented, but broke men and women. It takes years of perfecting your craft and countless hours of preparation. It also takes sacrifice, discipline, commitment, strategizing and often a competent and reliable team.

For years I didn't know what my talents were. I was good at a lot of things but not great at any one thing. I was a fast track runner, but never the fastest one. I could harmonize but not sing well enough to be a lead singer. I had good rhythm when I danced, but could never remember steps in a dance class. I could draw better than the average person but not great enough for my pieces to be displayed in a gallery and I could crochet but could never complete a whole blanket. It was hard for me to pinpoint my talents because they weren't physical and neither were they similar to the talents of the other kids or teens around me.

Then one day I realized that the way my brain worked WAS my talent. I could read people very well. I could pinpoint someone's insecurities as well as aspirations from a casual conversation. I knew what people wanted before they asked and being able to quickly analyze them always kept me one step ahead. *I was great at solving problems.* I was great at connecting the dots and finding the missing pieces so I could offer quick solutions to the problems that most people faced. I was also good at coherently putting my thoughts on paper for most readers to comprehend. Naturally, being a life coach and author made sense for me because it came effortlessly. Once I discovered my true talents and embraced them, then I was able to make a living off of it.

"When my finances lined up with my passion, I knew I found my gift".

START WITH THE END IN MIND

Even if you can't see the end, it's more important to just get started. It's better to start and make mistakes, rather than to just stand stagnant until you figure it out fully. Often times it's impossible to figure it out fully in theory just by "planning", it's in the "doing" process that you'll learn the most. You will fail at some things but that doesn't mean you're a *failure.* You're only a failure if you quit because you haven't learned from those mistakes!

LESSON 8: Failing isn't the opposite of success; it's a part of success.

"Think bigger sweetie" is what one of my mentors James Cannon often said to me. Now that notion is indented in me. I think that most people are afraid of dreaming big because that comes with the possibility of failing big and the fear of failure is the number one fear for millions of people. But the truth is that you can't accomplish anything without first thinking about it. No one who is great ever became great without first thinking that they COULD and WOULD be great. If you are uncomfortable picturing yourself doing great things and you are afraid to even imagine yourself at the pinnacle of success, you will *never* get there. I challenge you to think big, and then even bigger. Condition yourself to thinking bigger than your circumstances.

"Dreams are made one size bigger so that we can grow into them".

NOTHING IS IMPOSSIBLE

"Nothing is impossible, just thinking makes it so" - Will Durant

My favorite quote is: "You can achieve the impossible, just break it into possible steps".

I love it so much that I designed a miniature goal board of myself surrounded by people who inspire me. I typed the quote on there and carried it on my keychain for years. It was a constant reminder of the direction that I wanted to head in

DREAM SHOPPING

Some people call it *Window Shopping;* I call it *Dream Shopping.* You don't have to wait until you are able to afford the finer things in life to start looking at them. I encourage you to go out and look at those things you want (but can not afford now); grow your appetite. In fact, It's seeing those things that you want and being surrounded by those things that you wish to have someday that will actually encourage you to work even harder to acquire them.

Google some realtors in your area and see if any are

willing to show you some listings of houses in nice neighborhoods. Even if you don't have a pre-approval letter from a bank yet, don't let that stop you from taking the first step. You can even get dressed up one morning and take a ride through a really nice neighborhood and look out for "for sale" signs. Call the realtor's number on the sign in the yard and schedule a walk through of the property. If you're *really* lucky you may see a sign in the yard with a date and time that says "open house". If so, come back on that date and time and you'll be able to go inside the house and browse around.

You can schedule to test drive your dream car, schedule a campus visit of the college you aspire to go to, walk through the building you hope to open a business in one day or even stand on the stage in an auditorium that you vision yourself giving a speech from. Your brain can't distinguish if there are people in the room, or if the room is empty. All it captures is how you feel when you are envisioning that room full of people as you give your powerful speech. It's that passion, excitement and that rush of adrenalin that is going to cement that experience in your subconscious and help it to bring you those things that you want.

LIST OF PERSONAL DEVELOPMENT BOOKS

7 Habits of Highly Effective People
48 Laws of Power
As a Man Thinketh
Awaken the Giant Within
Born to Win
Eat That Frog
How Successful People Think
How to Win Friends and Influence People
Live Your Dreams
Outliers
The Secret
The Secret to Success
The Strangest Secret
The Success Principles
The Magic of Thinking Big
The Power of Now
The Power of Positive Thinking
Who Moved My Cheese?

Some of the authors of these books have multiple books; so make sure to look for their other books. Submerge yourself into any books in the following categories that you can get your hands on: sales, public speaking, marketing, advertising, branding, networking (including social networking), financial literacy, residual income and taxes. *Keep in mind that you can listen to a lot of audio books for free on YouTube.*

Chapter 2

Find Out What You Want

FIND OUT WHAT YOU WANT

<u>LESSON 9</u>: Most people don't get what they want because they simply don't know what they want

A lot of people don't know what they want, some people *know* what they want but don't know how to get it, and others know what they want and *how* to get it but they don't have enough drive or courage to go out and make it happen. Which one are you?

"There are winners, there are losers and there are people who have not yet learned how to win". – Les Brown

What do you love to do? Why do you love to do it? What excites you? What inspires you? Who do you admire? Where do you ultimately see yourself? How can you get there? What do you deserve? Why do you deserve it? What do you daydream about? What would you do if you know you couldn't fail? What would you want to do every single day, even if you weren't getting paid to do it?

Often times, it's not the fact that people are lazy that hinders them from going after their dream job or living their dream life. It's often the fact that they don't know what they want. They don't know what they're passionate about because they're bombarded by too many options or too many outside influences and just don't know where to start. The goal is to narrow down your focus to just one thing. In order to narrow down your focus you have to clear the clutter from your mind. So grab a pen to capture your thoughts on paper, and then start rearranging them until a clear plan emerges.

"Ideas grow wings if not written down immediately"   *−Baje Fletcher*

DISCOVER YOUR PASSION

1. Find a tranquil spot and take some deep breaths. With each breath you release, imagine yourself breathing out the clutter and breathing in clarity.

2. For five whole minutes I want you to try and think about absolutely nothing. Just allow your mind to relax.

3. Now, allow your mind to wander to the times before you were trained and tamed. Go back in time to your childhood when possibilities were limitless! Think about your favorite memories.

Think about what used to light you up. Think about the things you loved to do. When you played "pretend" what did you pretend to be?

4. Try to remember what your answer was when people asked you what you'd like to be when you grew up. Then think about school...whether it was elementary, middle school, high school or college. What kind of fieldtrips did you get the most excited about? What were your favorite subjects or what did you choose to major in and why? (*If you chose a certain major because someone else wanted you to or because you were trying to make someone else happy then that doesn't count*).

5. As children, we were all passionate about something before grownups told us what we couldn't do and who we couldn't be, through their limited and tainted view of the world. Sadly, most kids are negatively labeled or reprimanded for just being who they were meant to be; and as a result end up following in the same mediocre footsteps of who ever raised them. This question may sound odd, but what did you get in trouble for as a child? Did they say you talked too much? Perhaps you'd be great at sales. Did you cross-dress? Maybe you'd be a great clothing designer? Did you do

more daydreaming in class than paying attention to your work? Perhaps you'd have a great career in the marketing and advertising field. *You see where I'm going with this.*

6. Five or ten years ago could you see yourself living the life that you're living today? Are you way ahead? Right on track? Did you fall behind? Or have you just never planned your life that far ahead in intricate details.

7. What are some of the things that you *think* are holding you back? Lack of education, having children or dependents, being married? Etc.

8. If those things were not holding you back, what would your life be like? (Write it out in detail). What would your daily schedule be like? How would you feel? Where would you go? What would you do to earn a living?

9. If you were rich beyond your imagination what is the one thing you would not only enjoy, but also look forward to doing everyday? (Write it down...no matter how silly it may sound). Start thinking of your hobbies. You'd be surprised at how many things you do just for enjoyment that could actually bring in money if you looked at it from an occupational point of view.

10. Trace your family tree. Find out if there were any wildly successful members of your family and what it was that they were successful at. They may have left you clues. Oftentimes family members excel at the same things.

11. Have people ever told you that you were good at something in particular? Write down all of the things family, friends, or even strangers said you were good at. If more than three people told you that you were good at one of those things, then Google some ways to make money off of that and start reading books and seeking mentors in that field.

12. Call ten people who are close to you and ask them what do they think you're good at. Even ask them what are some things you need to work on. *(But only do so when you are absolutely prepared to take the criticism without taking offence). In order to get better you have to first hear the truth, embrace it no matter how bad it hurts and then make adjustments).*

THE LETTER THAT SAVED MY LIFE

About 6 or 7 years ago, after reading a self-help book, the author said to ask a few of your closest friends some things you need to work on. And so I sent out a mass text. Within a few minutes all the friends I reached out to responded...except one. They all sent me back a quick text with one or two things I needed to work on. The last friend didn't respond until the next day. But he sent me a long email that a lot of thought and love went into. It changed my entire perspective on life and people. It changed the way I thought about my potential, my future and myself. It played a huge part in molding me into the happy, helpful & hopeful woman that I am today. It read:

The Good:

By faaaaaar, the best thing about you is your intelligence and decisiveness. You have an uncanny ability to adapt intellectually (although not characteristically) to any environment. You're an excellent work ethic role model because you're an incredibly smart and hard worker. If you believe you can do something you take anyone's "no" as "not right now but try again later until you get a YES from me." :-) You're accomplished, daring and of excellent moral character...where it counts.

The Bad:

You teeter between unhappy and miserable only allowing for brief moments of satisfaction (never happiness). And the root of that misery is your own perception of people and life in general. You subconsciously sabotage any real chance at joy in your life because you can't allow yourself to be happy because you can't let go of past pain. That is also why you can't find purpose in life.

You lack the courage to address your issues and release them, allowing you to be an INCREDIBLE good symbol for women everywhere. You must take the time to address your own issues before your PERCEPTION continually ruins and runs away everything good away from you.

(& just when I braced myself for the "ugly" part, along came...)

The Beautiful:

You're passionate, loving, brave, admirable, loyal, honest, a humanitarian, real and soulfully beautiful. You have an incredible capacity to love and if you only adjust your PERCEPTION, you are one of the few individuals in this world that has been so gifted that could make a REAL DIFFERENCE!! You know EXACTLY what the solutions to your issues, problems, and hang-ups are you just lack the bravado to commit to them. In fact, I'm not telling you anything you don't already know... You just feel better reading it from someone else instead of facing it for yourself. Hope this helps. Love You.

This letter not only pointed out what I needed to work on, but it also gave me hope and a glimpse of who I could be, if I committed myself to work on those things. Hopefully you too have people in your life who love you enough to give you honest feedback. In the mean time continue to dig within to discover your passion.

13. If you don't know what you're passions are or what you excel at, then make a list of new things that you'd like to try and start experimenting over the course of the next few weeks. This may mean switching your college major, or picking up a trade.

14. You can even try and find it through the process of elimination. Make a list of things you do NOT like, then start working backwards and use that list as a guide. E.g. If you don't like to read don't start a profession that requires a lot of reading. Or if you hate math, don't pick a major that requires many math classes.

15. Ask other people about their passions. If you don't have access to them, then research and read about their passions. It may inspire or ignite something in you. *I have a friend who is a scientist and when I asked him why he chose the field of science he immediately lit up! His eyes*

widened, he sat up straighter and a smile surfaced on his face. He said. I love science because it's like magic! I love how you can mix two chemicals together and it turns into something else instantaneously. Or how a simple solution can lower someone's blood pressure or save their life. It's just fascinating!" He spoke with such eloquence and enthusiasm, that if I didn't already know what I was passionate about, science sounded like it was worth a shot.

16. Surround yourself with people who already found & embraced their passion.

LESSON 10: Changing your environment will change your state of mind, and changing your state of mind will change your life.

17. Shake things up a bit! Get yourself out of the norm and find other circles to mingle in. Expose yourself to new things on purpose. Make a mission to find five people who are completely different from you and hang out with them. Embrace a huge age gap, different religion, political view, or another race or culture. You'll never know what you can learn from them until you start learning.

18. Try things you normally wouldn't; visit places that you normally wouldn't. Google things to do in your city and try them no matter how different or weird they seem. You may like it!

DEVELOP YOUR TALENT INTO A SKILL

"Life's greatest gift is to find your talent early enough so you can develop it into skill"
—Baje Fletcher

While reading the biographies of very successful people, I found a few things that they all had in common. However, one thing stood out the most. Most of them knew what they wanted to be at an early age. Beyoncé for instance, said she was six when her parents took her to her first Michael Jackson concert and from that night on, she knew that she wanted to be an entertainer, just like her newfound idol.

If someone can decide what they want to be when they're six years old, then their chances of becoming that thing and being successful is magnified. If you have children, encourage them to find their calling while they're young. Take them to the opera, to museums, to concerts and to see plays in theatres. Take them to "bring your child to work" days and make a conscious effort to find ways to ignite their imagination. Tell your children about your mentors, heroes and idols and how they inspired you and what they taught you. They may also inspire them as well. Imagine how far your kids can go with your wisdom combined with their youth!

If your child doesn't know his or her calling yet, sit your child down look him or her in the eye and tell them that they are special...often. Tell them that they are meant for greatness and that they can do absolutely anything that they put their minds too. Don't think that children have to be a certain age to understand or appreciate your advice or encouragement. Even if you don't believe it, say it until you do, or say it until your child believes it. Even if they "act" uninterested, still encourage them. They'll thank you later. The only limitations placed upon their pliable minds are your own.

LESSON 11: It takes 10,000 hours of practice to reach mastery level in any field.

MAMA SYBLE

I was a young girl when I found myself staring at my reflection with a frown on my face. My grandmother glimpsed my expression out of the corner of her eye and asked me what was wrong. I had my hands on my collarbone that was protruding from my shoulders. I replied, "I hate how skinny I am, look how my bones sticks out". She looked puzzled but she took a few steps closer and touched my little hands that were trying to hide my collarbone. She said:

"Child! There is nothing wrong with you. Have you ever looked at the super models on the runway? That's how all their collarbones stick out. You belong on somebody's runway".

My eyes lit up as I straightened my back and squared up my shoulders; an air of confidence enclosed me. *Wow,* I thought to myself, *Mama Syble really believed I could be a model!* That very day, she sat around her sewing machine and sewed a dress for me. The dress seemed a few sizes too big, but she assured me that that was the latest style on the runways in Paris. As I tried it on and walked past that very same mirror I did a few hours prior...I looked the same but I felt differently. I felt like a million bucks. *Be careful of the words you use when speaking to children because your words can lift them to heights or lead them to destruction.*

LESSON 12: Words hold the power of death as well as life.

Because of her encouragement, what I once saw as a negative became a positive. As soon as I turned eighteen I pursued a fulltime career in modeling, which I was successful at for years.

"The tongue is strong enough to mend or break a heart"   -Baje Fletcher

For years I didn't know what my talents were. I was good at a lot of things but wasn't great at anything. I was fast in track & field, but wasn't one of the fastest on my team. I could harmonize, but couldn't sing well enough to be a lead singer. I had good rhythm when I danced, but could never remember steps in a dance class. I could draw better than the average person, but not great enough for my pieces to be displayed in a gallery. And I could crochet but not good enough for me to complete a whole blanket. It was hard for me to pinpoint my talents because they weren't physical; neither were they similar to the talents of the other kids or teens around me.

But one day something clicked. I realized that the way my brain worked WAS my talent. I could read people very well. I could pinpoint people's insecurities as well as aspirations from a casual conversation. I knew what people wanted before they asked and being able to quickly analyze them always kept me one step ahead. *I was great at solving problems.* I was great at connecting the dots and finding the missing pieces so I could offer quick solutions to the problems that most people faced. I was also good at capturing my thoughts and observations and coherently putting on paper. Naturally, being a life coach and author made sense for me because it came effortlessly and it just felt right. Once I uncovered my true talents, embraced them and polished them into skills, then I was able to make a living off of them.

YOUR ENVIRONMENT DICTATES YOUR FUTURE

You are learning things all the time; you have to teach yourself *what you want to learn*... Analyze your life. Think about the environment where you hang out, the places you run your errands, and the people you hang out with. After analyzing each, is there is anything or anyone you can substitute in order to enhance your life, or make you more successful. If your problem is that you keep meeting the wrong kind of people, perhaps it's *where* you choose to go out. Perhaps you meet people randomly when you're pumping gas, grocery shopping, or having lunch at local restaurants. In most cases you can upgrade the caliber of people you meet just by changing your daily routine. Instead of running errands and shopping in your own neighborhood, take a ten-minute drive and shop on the more sophisticated side of town. Plus, sometimes by stepping into unfamiliar territory, it gives you a new outlook on life. When you're in a neighborhood where the grass is greener, the flowers are brighter, the air is crisper and people are friendly, you'll have a better perspective on life in general. I understand that everything may cost a little bit more in the nicer neighborhoods, but the relationships you'll make and the doors that may open for you will be well worth the extra dollars. It can be something as simple as changing the park where you go jogging. The extra ride may be worth it if you use those opportunities to network. You may not meet people on the first few trips but don't let that deter you. Don't be afraid to start conversations and ask questions. Don't be afraid to exchange business cards and ask your newfound friends if they can send you a text message if they hear of any social or business events. Even reading the community boards at coffee shops, churches, supermarkets and libraries in other neighborhoods may provide some beneficial leads as well. (PS. unless they ask, you don't have to mention that you're from the "other" side of town either).

ONLY YOU CAN LIVE YOUR LIFE

"There is nothing worse than regret's lingering taste". – *Baje Fletcher*

I've spoken to so many people who are stuck in careers that they absolutely hate. And when I asked them why didn't they pursue something else they were passionate about, I usually got one of two answers. Either:

1.They were trying to please their parents or

2.They didn't think that they could make money pursuing their passion.

Neither are good reasons to neglect pursing what you love. Your parents may have your best interest at heart but they can't live your life for you. You are the one, and the only one, who'll have to forever live with the regret of turning your back on your dream. What was the best route for your parents may not necessarily be the best route for you; and you have to be strong enough to let them know that. Sure it will disappoint them, but it will do you more psychological and emotional damage than you can imagine, trying to live a life you that hate. Don't do it.

Life can be one long dull ride when you're not doing what you love. Whatever it is that lights you up, there are many ways to make money off of it. Your immediate goal in life should to be researching those ways.

"Have the courage to follow your heart & intuition. They somehow know what you truly want to become" – Steve Jobs

SELF EDUCATION IS KEY

"The more you learn, the more you earn"
– Frank Clark

It's a proven fact that people who are educated get what they want more easily than people who aren't. When I say educated, I'm not only speaking of formal or institutional education. I know many people who don't have any degrees but they know a lot more than people who have their Bachelors and even Masters degree. I'm speaking of self-education. Education should be a life long process and shouldn't end when you walk across a stage and receive a piece of paper. That should only be the beginning actually. Maybe I take education so seriously because I was raised in a country where a high school education wasn't free. It really bothers me when I see how easy it is to get educated in America yet so many people don't take the time to do so even though it may cost them nothing! So many teens drop out of high school and so many fail to research scholarships and grants in order to attend college because of sheer laziness! There are so many grants and scholarships available to those who just go looking! And in a lot of cases your grades aren't the deciding factor. I've seen thousands of dollars given away through scholarships; and in some cases you may qualify just by being a single mother. Some organizations will even award you money just for being of a certain ethnicity or having certain color eyes, and there are a lot of scholarships solely based on financial hardship and all you have to do is write an essay saying why you need funding.

LESSON 13: Education is a life long journey.

Education shouldn't stop after high school or even college. You have a duty to educate yourself for life and you can only do so by constantly seeking knowledge. You can be knowledgeable and not necessarily formally educated. Getting an education is usually a four-year task. Staying knowledgeable is lifetime process. Many multimillionaires never graduated from college. But they were knowledgeable enough to acknowledge what they didn't know, and hire the people who knew more than they did in particular subject matters. You can seek knowledge not only through reading and listening to audiobooks, but by seeking mentors, watching tutorials, joining teleseminars, webinars and by attending seminars and workshops.

"Formal education makes you a living but self education will make you a fortune" – Jim Rohn

Until you have enough money to get a formal education or to learn a trade, you can teach yourself. You can find books at the library, you can go to a bookstore and read books there for free (as long as you don't leave the store with them) and you can look up free YouTube videos and hear what others have to say on any subject.

Most higher learning institutions give you the option to "test out" of classes. Which means, you could read the textbook on your own time and pay a flat fee (which is usually lower than the price of the class), and then take the test for that class. If you pass that test you would get credit for that particular class. The official name of that program is (CLEP) The College-Level Examination Program® it helps you receive college credit for what you already know, for a fraction of the cost of a college course. Developed by the College Board, CLEP is the most widely accepted credit-by-examination program, available at more than 2,900 colleges and universities.

Some schools (even some ivy league schools) will allow you and your children to attend for free if you work on campus, (even if you have a cleaning job, you would still qualify).

"An investment in knowledge always pays the best interest" — *Benjamin Franklin*

MOTIVATIONAL SPEAKERS

I've read many books throughout my life and listened to many seminars from the best motivational speakers, and though their delivery and speaking style may differ, most of their core messages on how to be successful have stood the test of time. Motivational speakers force you to analyze your life, they help you to discover the direction that you need to be headed in and most importantly they motivate you and push you in that direction. If you don't have any mentors or you find it hard to secure their time, then listening to motivational speakers is the next best thing. You can start by reading their books and then listening to their seminars on their website or YouTube until you are able to go see them speak live! Some of the speakers I find captivating and inspirational are, Tony Robbins, Les Brown, Jack Canfield, Eric Thomas, John Maxwell, Joel Osteen, Lisa Nichols, Tyrese Gibson, Suze Orman, Iyanla Vanzant and Steve Harvey. Jim Rohn and Zig Ziglar are two great speakers as well. Even though you can't see them live (because they've passed away) you can still watch all their speaking engagements online.

MAKE A MENTOR MAP

Write down the names of some people who you admire and who inspire you. Then write down what they did or are doing that has had that positive impact on you mentally. Write down a few questions that you would ask them if you had ten minutes of their undivided attention. Now write down some things that they could assist you with if they were actually willing. Perhaps you could gain invaluable knowledge in your field if you worked under them, interned for their company, if they invited you to some networking functions or they introduced you to some people you could potentially do business with. Finally, make a list of your good qualities, talents, skills, trades, education and resources. Once you have your lists together make it your mission to seek out your mentors. You may reach some of them; you may not. But you have nothing to lose, so give it your best shot! Chances are, they have a website that lists their email address, or they may a have social media account where you can send them a message, or they may have a company that's listed publicly and you can leave a message with their secretary. Be creative! If you do make contact, let them know what you can offer them in exchange for them agreeing to mentor you.

LESSON 14: Give before you expect to receive.

YOU HAVE TO SPEAK UP

LESSON 15: Knowing what you want is a start, but you have to be able to articulate to others what you want in order to get it.

You have to speak up to get what you want ---point-blank-period. That was something I had to learn the hard way. I hated to look people straight in the eye when we were one-on-one, and that never went over well. Because ever since I was a child people use to say if I couldn't look them in the eye it was because I was hiding something. That wasn't the case; looking people in their eyes just made me uncomfortable...because I was shy, and it was really nothing deeper than that. For years I was in the same room with many influential people that I could have worked with, partnered with or became friends with but I didn't act in that moment; at that time I was too afraid to step out of my comfort zone.

"How you carry yourself is the first indication of how people get to treat you"

I hated to speak in front of a room of people and I hated to have all eyes on me. But I was also growing weary of being unassertive and waiting until it was "my turn" because often times "my turn" never came. One pivotal day I realized that what I hated even more than being stared at...was being "overlooked". I got tired of opportunities passing me by because I didn't speak up or speak up quickly. I got tired of missing out because I didn't introduce myself to anyone in the room or because I walked in a room and automatically took the chair in a corner or in the back instead of sitting in the front as if I belonged there. Do you know how many chances I had to properly position myself but didn't? Countless. Worst of all sometimes people misinterpreted my shyness for being "stuck up" or antisocial.

"Shy people notice everything, but they don't get noticed".

LESSON 16: Closed mouths don't get fed.

You not only have to know what you want, but you have to know how to express to others what you want so you can convince them to help you. You have to paint the exact picture of the vision that you see in your head to them. You have to be able to see your vision all the way through so you can explain it to them step by step. It has been stated that public speaking is most people's number one fear. Master that fear and you'll be a step ahead of most. I remember the most excruciating part of my college years; it was at the beginning of every new semester. With each new semester came a new class, a new professor and a whole new set of students that I had to stand up in front of and introduce myself to. I absolutely, positively hated it. My heart would beat at a double pace the moment the first few students got up and introduced themselves. The countdown began. My mouth would get dry and I'd start to sweat. I always got so nervous and wondered if everyone else had such a hard time or was there something wrong with me? Eventually I made a choice to face my fear. As an elective class I chose "Public Speaking" the following semester. Was it nerve racking? Absolutely! But I wanted to get over this thing that had such a grip on me. In that public speaking class we had to write our own speeches and then go in front of the class and read them, at other times we had to tell a story. The writing part was always easy for me; it was when I had to convey what was on paper to the whole classroom that I got all chocked up. I must say I was horrible at speaking. Period. I would look up or at a wall or I'd look at anything but the people who were right in front of me. I had a thick Jamaican accent that I could not control and it flew out whenever it felt like it. I'd stutter and eat half of my words from trying to read too fast when I was nervous. But the more I did it, the easier it got. Here is how I was able to get better at speaking and I'm sure it will work for you as well.

- Remind yourself that they are just people like yourself.

- Take long breaths. Don't rush; take your time.

- Instead of trying to read or memorize every word, just make bullet points. Perhaps one word or one sentence that reminds you about the story or the subject you want to talk about and then tell that part of the story by memory. It will sound more natural.

- Look people in their eyes, just as if you are having a normal conversation.

- Start by saying what you are going to talk about, then talk about it and then sum up what you just talked about.

- It never hurts to make a little joke or reference something that made you laugh, because chances are, it will make others laugh as well.

- Don't take yourself too seriously. Making a joke about yourself would lighten the load.

- You don't have to stand in one spot, if strolling along the stage feels more natural then do that.

- Take a public speaking class or join Toastmasters International.

- Enroll in public competitions (like pageants or debate teams) so you'll have no choice but to perform.

LESSON 17: Success leaves clues.

Today, those clues are easier than ever to find. Those clues are in books, videos, tutorials, seminars and workshops so you have no excuse. Anything that you want to know is literally at your fingertips! If you want to find out ways to make residual income you can search it on Google, if you want to find a local book club you can Google it, if you want to find jobs where you can work from home, you can search it on the internet. Literally, ANYTHING you want to find is just a keystroke away. If you are one of the very few who doesn't have Internet or a computer, you can always go to the library. There is absolutely no reason why in this day and age you can't be successful. If you don't know where to start, type in something as simple as this in your search engine or on YouTube "How can I make more money?" and you'll have plenty of options....

"Success is waiting for you, all you have to do is go looking for it and it will meet you half way".

You don't have to always have every minute detail planned and you don't have to always know what you are looking for...just start looking. By doing so, the universe will help things align in your favor. For instance, when people see you *trying*, they are more compelled to help you as opposed to you just *talking* about what you want to do. You don't always have to see what is at the end of the road, just trust your instincts and run as far as you can see, run as far as the light will take you and trust that when you get there that light will shine a little further.

YOU CAN'T BE AFRAID TO ASK

You can't be afraid to ask for what you want, whether it is a raise, a promotion, a gift, quality time, whatever it is that you need, you can't be afraid to ask for it, and more importantly, you can't be afraid to walk away if your boss or partner or whoever isn't willing to give you what you think you deserve. That goes for the workforce, as well as your personal life. I've noticed that it's the same people who are afraid to ask for a raise or afraid to speak up at their jobs, who are also afraid to discuss with their partner what they need from them in their relationship...and they consequently don't get it.

If you aren't happy with something, but you continue to accept it, then nothing is going to change. As a life coach, you have no idea how many people express to me that they aren't happy at their jobs or in their relationships and not only are they still there but they never express their concerns to their boss or partner. People will hate how they're being treated but they won't say anything about it, or they'll complain to everyone else around them *except* the one person who is misusing them...which isn't going to get anything solved.

Speak up! If you aren't happy then say something. Life is just too short to be miserable. If you feel like you are being overlooked or shortchanged (whether financially or emotionally), think about all the things you've been through, all the sacrifices that you've made, all the opportunities that you already missed out on and make a promise to yourself to never accept that treatment again. If you voice your concerns and nothing changes then it's time to leave. You can't be afraid to walk away, because if you don't, then that person will know that they can continue to treat you anyway they wish without any consequences; and that's exactly what they'll do.

<u>SELL YOURSELF</u>

The fear of speaking up really stems from a fear of rejection. The best way to get over that is to keep getting rejected. I know that sounds insane but it really is the only solution. So...about that person you have a crush on...just pick up the phone, dial their number and invite them out. About your product that you want to get in stores...Google a list of stores in your area, call and speak to a manager and find out the process to get your product on their shelves. So about those sales you need to make at your job...make it a competition between you and a co-worker to see who can sell the most.

LESSON 18: Nothing gets you over the fear of rejection faster than cold calling.

The fastest way to get over your fear of rejection is to get a sales job cold calling people, or doing door-to-door sales. It will be terrifying, nerve racking and absolutely worth it. Because the people who get what they want in this world are the people who can sell themselves.

Study what makes the greats...great! Go on YouTube and watch video clips of the world's greatest speakers delivering the world greatest speeches.

Take initiative, you don't have to wait until you're called on. When someone asks if anyone would like to lead the group in prayer, or take roll call, or make the announcements, just volunteer. The more you speak up, the better you'll get at speaking.

Don't expect anyone to do your job...even if you pay them; because no one can sell you, your product or your service like you. Start practicing selling yourself. Realize that even if you don't have a company or a product of your own, you're still into "sales". You're selling yourself to strangers in hopes of making friends, you're selling yourself to friends in hopes of finding a life-long partner, you're selling yourself to schools in order to get accepted or you're selling yourself to potential employers in hopes of landing the job; so you might as well perfect the craft.

ASK FOR WHAT YOU WANT

We live in a society where everyone is out for themselves and self-interest prevails. In this social tug of war it's usually the wealthy and powerful (ten percent of the population) that comes out on top, while the masses are left to fight for the scraps that are left behind. It *seems* like taxes, rules, laws and policies all work in the favor of the 'elite', however this isn't true. It's not that the ten percent are better or more deserving than everyone else; but they are many steps ahead because they're armed with the most powerful weapon that a man can possibly have: *knowledge*...and they aren't afraid to use it.

There are many legal loopholes, shortcuts and perks available to us all; most people are just unaware of them. *Knowledge* is what separates those who live easier lives from those who struggle to make ends meet. *Knowledge* that has been passed down from parents, grandparents and mentors; in addition to information acquired through years of schooling, through books and from exercising social intelligence. Once you have knowledge, you have to activate it by asking for what you want and negotiating things on your terms.

Most of the time, companies aren't going to offer to lower the prices on their products and services. You have to *ask*. Ask for referral fees, coupons, discounts, vouchers and credits to have the price lowered. Ask if there are any specials or promotions that they're currently running; or if they offer any payment plans, layaway plans, any discounts for kids, seniors, government workers, or employees of the corporation you're currently working for. Ask if you're a member of an association like AAA or a frequent flyer club if you're eligible for any discounts. Don't be afraid to ask them to match a competitor's price or for a perk or discount for being a loyal customer. And no it's not begging, or being desperate, it's being "smart". Too much pride gets you nowhere. You deserve to save every cent you earn, because it's *your* money.

When you aren't able to get what you need from one company, it's okay to ask for a referral, or ask if they know of another company that can better service your needs. You'd be surprised to see how many people are willing to help if you only ask. Keep in mind that many times better offers are given to *current* customers, so if you know someone who's already a customer, then try to partner with that person. If you have a friend that is an employee of that company, he may be able to use *his* friends and family discount.

There are plenty of shortcuts and loopholes that you can take advantage of: *First,* you have to know that they exist. *Secondly,* you have to be willing to go out there and look for them. *Thirdly,* you have to be able to speak up, voice your concerns and ask for what you want. I see too many hard working individuals getting the short end of the stick because they are afraid to speak up. Sometimes a simple Google search of free offers in your area, or coupons for a certain store can save you money.

ATLANTIS

When I went to Dubai for my birthday, I Googled "Free things to do in Dubai", and found that if it was my birthday I could go to the Atlantis water park for free. By the time I saw that offer I was a day late but I still printed out the pass and went to the park. I asked one of the attendants if there was anyway I could still use it...and she told me no. I then asked for a supervisor; she told me that the supervisor was going to tell me the same thing, but I told her I was willing to take my chances. When the supervisor arrived I told her that I know it expired yesterday but *"as a courtesy"* is there anyway she could make an exception and let me in the park anyway...and she did! I was able to enjoy all the rides, slide through the shark tank and have a blast the rest of the day. So you see, it doesn't hurt to ask, you just have to ask the person who has the power to make the decisions.

BAHAMAS BOUND

Flight 221 from Bahamas to the US was delayed three hours. I was extremely agitated because I was in a hurry to get back home for a meeting right after my flight. I obviously wasn't making it anymore. Everyone else on the flight was annoyed just as I was, but after the flight arrived everyone else forgot about the last three hours of inconvenience...not me. I value my time and if I'm delayed for a reason that's no fault of my own, I want to be properly compensated. So right before I boarded the flight, I asked for a manager so I could get some kind of refund or voucher for future travel, for the delay that caused me to miss my meeting. I was told that a manager wasn't available at the moment but I was given an email address. I quickly sent an email right from my phone as I was boarding. Within a week a new ticket arrived in my mailbox for a future trip to Bahamas.

FLYING FIRST CLASS

I remember sitting in the airport waiting for boarding to begin for my flight on American Airlines. I glanced at my ticket in my hand. They had me sitting in the middle row...I hate the middle row and wanted a window. Right when I was about the approach the counter to ask the agent if it was possible to switch seats, my eyes wandered to the information board for that flight. It read:

0 passengers on the standby list.
0 passengers on the upgrade list.

A light bulb went off in my head. If there was no one waiting to be upgraded to first class maybe I should try. I walked up to the agent at the counter, he was a 6 foot tall grumpy looking male. No smile and no greeting. He just continued typing away and doing whatever it is that he was doing before I approached him. I said, "Hi, is it possible to get a window seat or get upgraded to first class?" He asked: "Are you Elite status?" I paused then said, "No...not on this airline". He asked, then why would you get upgraded?" Hesitantly I replied, "I don't know, I was just asking". He agreed to give me just a window seat and gave me the new ticket without even making any eye contact. "Thanks", I muttered, as I slowly walked back to my seat with my shoulders slumped. I looked at the ticket as I sat down; it had a big F on it, F for first class. I smiled and mouthed "Thank You" to him. He winked at me and continued typing away.

CASINO ROYALE

Another example, on one of my trips to Italy I decided to go to Switzerland for the day. I heard about a huge casino there and wanted to check it out before I had to catch a flight back to the US the next day. It was only an hour train ride from Milan (where I was at the time) so I went for it. I played blackjack for a few hours ...and lost all the cash I had on me. So I went to the ATM to pull out more money ...but the machine took my card! I don't know what happened, it didn't even ask me for my pin number; it just swallowed my card and didn't spit it back out! That was my only card and I didn't have any more cash. I was stuck in some strange land by myself, and though the country had four national languages, English wasn't one of them. I don't speak German, French, Italian or Romansh and I didn't have any cash or cards to buy a ticket back to Milan so I could catch my flight back to the US that was leaving in eight hours. I panicked for a few seconds. Then I started muttering under my breath: *"Think Baje think, think Baje think."* I walked up to one of the tellers and explained my situation to her. She replied "espeske-no-inglish". Oh crap. I asked "Manager?" She went in the back and within five minutes came out with an English speaking man in a suit. I told him that the ATM took my card and he told me that the casino didn't service the machines so I'd have to wait until the banks open in the morning to see what they could do. I told him that by the time the banks open I'd have to be on a flight. He said that he was sorry, but he really couldn't do anything to physically get back the card. Then there was silence *(think Baje think)*. If I accepted his gracious "No", I would have had to find a way back to Milan, Italy (the next country over) risk missing my flight and would have had to book a whole new ticket back to America...over something that wasn't even my fault. I've seen ATMs take cards after putting in the wrong pin code, but this machine didn't even ask me for a pin. This was totally unacceptable. *(Think Baje think).* I said: "Sir, I live in America and this is my first time here. A good friend of mine who used to live here spoke very highly of this place and I took his recommendation. I'm here in this country by myself and I don't want to be stranded as a single woman. Is there any possible way *as a courtesy,* that the casino can give me back the few hundred I lost at the blackjack table, so I can book a ticket back to catch my flight?" Once again there was silence. I kept a straight face but my heart was beating louder than a Congo drum. He said "If I agree to this, you have to leave the casino immediately. You can't stay around and continue to gamble. I smiled and said; "Deal" We shook on it and within ten minutes he gave me back the money I lost. I was so excited to walk out that casino. I remember letting out a long sigh of relief while leaving and thinking: *WOW...anything is possible, if you only ASK.*

Those are just a few examples, but people have made exceptions over and over and over again for me, simply because I'm not afraid to ask. You should try it.

THE LAW OF ATTRACTION

LESSON 19: Intention is like a magnet.

The Law of Attraction is also known as *The Law of Vibration* and states that everything vibrates and nothing rests. Vibrations of the same frequency resonate with each other, so like attracts like energy.

"Be intentional about what you want and the law of attraction will bring it to you".

You are an extension of your thoughts; you are a reflection of your thoughts. How you dress, how you speak, whom you associate with, even where you work have all manifested from your thoughts. Whatever you keep in your dominant thought, is what you'll attract more of into your life. What you think about dictates your mood; your mood dictates the kind of energy you put out to others, and the type of energy you give is typically the kind of energy that you're given back. You argue with someone, they argue back. You apologize to someone, you'll more than likely get an apology back. You walk around with a grumpy face and no one will smile at you, but smile at someone and chances are they'll smile back. Ever heard the positive phrase "I'm on a roll!" or even the negative phrases. "When it rains, it pours" or "Misery loves company"? Well, that's exactly how the *Law of Attraction* works.

"Life is 10% what happens to you and 90% how you react to those things"

When you recognize a pattern of negative events, use that as a cue to adjust the way you are thinking. It may not be your thoughts that are attracting those things in your life, but the way you choose to deal with them plays a huge part. If you're aware of this commanding law then you can often break the cycle of negativity by changing your thoughts, changing your surroundings or changing those who surround you. Some of the most powerful things cannot be explained in words, but only in feelings; Like God, intuition and attraction. Unfortunately, sometimes it's not even you who is attracting negative things your way, but the people who you are surrounded by, so clean up your circle!

THE SUBCONSCIOUS

The conscious mind vs. the subconscious mind.

The conscious mind is the first layer of your mind and is responsible for logic and reasoning. It also controls the actions that you do intentionally.

The subconscious is the layer that defines you. It holds your values, beliefs and attitudes. It's the part of the mind that you're not fully aware of, but it influences your actions and feelings.

The subconscious mind is not easily accessible compared to the conscious mind because the memories lay in a deeper state.

LESSON 20: Words speak to your conscious mind but images, music and sounds speak to the subconscious.

Your mind is a filter, kind of like a Google search engine. Everything in the world is neutral, but it's our minds that give meaning to certain things and situations. Every second of the day, your mind filters everything around you. You label, judge and react to things based on how your mind is programed. You can choose to *see* and *attract* more of what you want if you become more in tuned with your subconscious.

Here are some ways to tap into and strengthen your subconscious:

Tap into your creativity. Practicing art, music, pottery or any other form of self-expression can help your subconscious to reveal itself. Allowing yourself to be creative can open up a side to your personality that was always there but you were unable to express.

Surround yourself with people you want to be like.

Watch what you say, what you think about and be careful of what you watch on TV...especially before you go to sleep.

Choose to think about positive and productive things. When you catch yourself thinking negative thoughts change them immediately.

Only speak of good things you want to come true. Don't speak of things that you don't want to occur.

When people are taking part in conversations that are negative or make you feel uncomfortable, change the subject.

Separate yourself from anyone or anything that makes you uneasy, (even if you don't have a specific reason why they make you feel that way). For example, if you are in a great mood, and all of a sudden when you hear from a certain person your whole mood changes...or you may be gambling and on a winning streak and as soon as that certain person comes around the table then your luck changes for the worst...separate yourself.

"In religion they call it spirits. In science they call it energy. In the streets they call it vibes. Whatever you call it...trust it"

Meditate or do yoga.

Schedule daily quiet time for yourself; no conversation, no music...just silence. Start with 30 minutes and then gradually work in more time. (Pay attention to your thoughts and self-talk during this time of reflection).

Reflect back on your childhood to the things your parents used to tell you, and see how they shaped your adulthood. Decipher which beliefs are actually yours and which ones were forced upon you. Start letting go of the ideologies that you no longer need, or the ones that do you no good.

Therapy isn't bad - we all have some type of baggage or some issues, some affect us subconsciously without us even knowing it, and if we don't know it's affecting us how can we fix it? Sometimes it takes someone from the outside looking in to point out our hang-ups. Sometimes it's not so much the advice that we need; sometimes we just need to hear ourselves talk, sometimes what we need is simply for someone to listen. In many cases we already know the answer and we just need reinforcement or someone to hold us accountable to do the right thing.

Follow your intuition. When you are trying to make a decision or are confronted with a problem, the very first thing that comes to your mind is probably your subconscious talking.

INSTINCT & INTUITION

...Learn to trust both.

Instinct: A natural impulse. A way of behaving, thinking or feeling that is not learned.

Intuition: The ability to understand something immediately, without the need for conscious reasoning.

Think of instincts as something you don't make a conscious choice about; you just do it quickly and naturally without thinking about it. And think of intuition as a feeling or a hunch about something that makes you lean towards something without knowing much about it...but you can still have enough time to make the choice to follow it or not.

LESSON 21: Your intuition is your sixth sense. Allow it to guide you.

Follow your feelings. Ever met a baby or dog that is friendly with everyone, but doesn't want to be near one specific person? Pay attention and act accordingly; it's not a coincidence. Ever strayed away from your daily routine, (like took an alternate way home or walked instead or driving) and on that particular day you missed a bad accident? Pay attention.

"Your instincts and intuition are your internal GPS"

Intuition can come in the form of suspicion, fear, sudden anxiety, or indecisiveness. It can come in the form of curiosity about a person, thing or event. It may be a nagging feeling that something just isn't right or you aren't being told the truth. It may come in the form of an impulsive feeling pressing you to do something for no apparent reason or a thought that you just can't seem to shake. It may be a strong pull to move in a certain direction. Some people say it's the way God or the spirit guides them, some say it feels like time is standing still when they're being guided by their intuition (kind of like when they slow down a part in a movie for dramatic effect when something big is about to happen). Whenever you get any of these feelings, get quiet (physically and figuratively speaking) and try to figure out what your intuition is telling you.

March 16, 2016 (A post a made on my Instagram account) @MissBaje

I was racing to my first meeting this morning, a man approached me & asked if I had any change so he could get something to eat. In a big city like New York this is beyond common. So I told him "sorry I can't today" ... he said "ok" & walked away. I walked to the next block to the building I had to go into but I couldn't shake the look in his eyes... and the way he asked me (he stood a few feet away like he didn't want to scare me off, I could tell that he still had his pride). Even though I was already late, something in me felt like I was allowing my blessing to walk away. Every once in a while I get that feeling ... (as if God sent him my way & is just waiting to see what I'm going to do) and those are the faces I remember forever if I walk away. I ran back down the block & chased this man down to give him some money. We held a brief conversation... he was Jamaican just like me. He said, "God sent you back, the spirit told you to come back". I just smiled. As I turned to walk away, he said, "Ma'am, I know you're late but I just want to say that you're a blessed child of God and may your guardian angel walk with you". I chased this homeless man down to bless him, but in turn, I was blessed. Because even though he was in one of the worst positions that a man could ever be in, his heart was not hardened. His words will forever resonate with me because he inspired me to continue on my mission to help millions.

"When your intuition compels you to do something...don't ask why...oblige and just do it" —Baje Fletcher

Chapter 3

Learn to "Unlearn"

LEARN TO "UNLEARN"

The inability to let go is what holds most people back. They're unable to let go of bitter memories, old principles, and bad habits. They hold their future hostage to their past, because they aren't willing to forgive those who did them wrong or "unlearn" the ways they've grown accustomed to doing things, even when it's detrimental to their mental, emotional and financial development.

YOU are what is holding you back and until you realize that and accept that, you won't have the power to set yourself free. Without going into too much detail, I will share that I've been neglected as a child, violated as a woman and manipulated as a mate, but I learned at a young age that though I couldn't control how people treated me, I WAS able to control how I reacted...and whatever reaction I *chose* is what paved the way for future events. I also knew that if I wanted to overcome any of the bad things that I went through then I couldn't accept any of my "excuses" no matter how justified they sounded. I had to take responsibility for everything that came in my life...both good and bad. I had to accept my share of responsibility in every situation that went wrong, and if it was someone that totally wronged me through no fault of my own, then I had to have the courage to forgive them.

"Forgiveness is not for the perpetrator, but it's a gift you give yourself in order to move on with your life"   *—Baje Fletcher*

Before you can move forward you have to address what's been holding you back all this time. Many times it's the beliefs that our parents raised us with that consciously or subconsciously keeps us from reaching our goals. Sometimes it's a case of sibling rivalry and in many cases it is past relationships with our exes. You have to claim your power. Life is all about choices. You are where you are now because of your choices...period. If something happened to you that was beyond your control, it's still a choice to let go of it today. Too many people bring the past with them to the future. You have every right to be bitter over some things that occurred in your life, however doing so would only hurt *you*. You can press the reset button on your life at *any time* and as many times as you need to.

LEARN TO TAKE RISKS

People spend too much time complaining about things that they can't change, or when it's things that they can change, (like working for an unpleasant boss); they often still don't change it. Most people will complain about the amount of their paycheck, but refuse to go out and look for another job. They'll complain about their dwindling finances but still won't make the effort to become financially literate. They'll complain about their responsibilities as parents but they chose to have kids before they were actually ready. They'll complain about how they're mate doesn't make them happy, but they'll stay cemented in unfulfilled marriages.

LESSON 22: In this ever-changing world, the biggest risk you can take is taking no risk at all.

The hardest thing for most people to do is to take risks. They ferociously cling to the bad hand that life deals them, rather than taking a chance on a new shuffle for fear of getting a hand that's worse. They rather be unhappy, than face the unknown.

JUMP BEFORE YOU'RE READY!

<u>LESSON 23:</u> It's impossible to get ahead by doing what everyone else is doing.

Stop waiting! Stop taking the route that everyone else takes and take the road less traveled. You can't wait until you're ready...you just have to jump! That's what makes the successful...successful! They don't wait for a perfect time, because they know that there will never be a perfect time! They ask themselves "If not now, then when?" and then they take that leap off the cliff and into the unknown. They know that someone who believes in them may never come along; they know that between bills, debt and other obligation they may never get enough saved...and so they jump courageously before they are ready!

"Courage isn't the absence of fear, it's the ability to act in the presence of fear"
—Bruce Lee

The successful jump even though everyone around them is telling them their idea is stupid, or crazy, or that things will never work. (Like Steve Harvey says) they jump and hope to God that their parachute opens on time. Often times, their parachute doesn't open on time on their first jump. They get bruised up, they get disappointed, they get embarrassed, they get bankrupted, their car gets repossessed or their house gets foreclosed on. They cry, get depressed or even isolate themselves for a while ... and then they jump again! And that's what makes them *different*.

LESSON 24: The number one trait & absolute requirement to be successful is resilience!

DON'T PROCRASTINATE

LESSON 25: Don't put off for tomorrow what you can do today.

One of the biggest flaws that we as people have is that we love to procrastinate. We tend to push our biggest task to the end of the list instead of tackling it first. "I'll just do it later, or tomorrow" is what we tell ourselves; then before you know it we miss our deadline or we're frantically scurrying at the last minute.

"No one word has stifled success more than the word: tomorrow"
−Baje Fletcher

Your day will go so much smoother if you get your biggest task out of the way first. Once it's behind you, you'll be less anxious, less stressed and more productive because you'll be able to think more clearly. "Swallow That Frog - 21 Great Ways to Stop Procrastinating and Get More Done in Less Time" is the title of a book that a friend of mine recommended that I read. She ranted about how much it helped her and she lived by it religiously. In fact, she has photos of frogs or frog toys and frog souvenirs strategically placed all around her house, her car and even in her wallet, to remind her to not postpone the things that she needs to do. Her strategy may seem a little weird, or drastic but she gets the job done, and in the end, that's what counts the most.

LEARN TO BE HAPPY

LESSON 26: If you give someone the power to make you happy then that person also has the power to make you sad.

You have to find yourself, for yourself. Find out what makes you smile, laugh or light up inside. When you know how to make yourself happy then you can start doing so. Too many people live their lives incomplete because they have been brainwashed to think that they are missing their other half. They miss out on *fully living* because they are *waiting*, waiting for Prince Charming or Princess Charmaine to come along and complete them. Personally, I think that notion is quite ridiculous! I think that most relationships don't work because people don't know themselves well enough as individuals, so they are relying on someone else to essentially build them. I feel that in order to build a solid foundation together, you must first have a solid foundation individually. You must know who you are, what you want, what makes you tick and what sets you off. It is very important that you know what your goals are, identify the things you need to work on, and then actually work on those things before you look for a mate. We all have baggage, but the key is to deal with it *or* unload that baggage prior to entering into a new relationship. Otherwise we'll lose our identity following someone else or we'll keep running into a wall of disappointment while expecting some poor soul to fix us.

First thing first...you have to **decide that you want to be happy.** It all starts with an unwavering decision. Most people say that they want to be happy, but if they're still holding on to things that make them sad then they don't *really* want to be happy.

Secondly...**realize that life doesn't owe you anything,** no one owes you anything, not the world, not your best friend, not your parents and certainly not

God. You have life...it's your job to make the best of it. If you have a sound mind, good health, your freedom and all your limbs you already have a head start in life.

Thirdly, if you live in the United States of America..."The Land of Opportunity", thank your parents because you already have an advantage over the rest in this world whose sole wish is to cross the ocean for a shot of the American dream. You live in one of the best countries in the world. Don't take it for granted! **Take advantage!**

A TASTE OF JAMAICA

My parents sent me to Jamaica to live with extended family when they divorced when I was six years old, and it wasn't until returning to the U.S. eight years later that I realized how poor the living conditions in Jamaica were. Nine of us lived in our house. At the first smell of rain, we use to strategically place pots and pans all over the house in their usual spots, in order to catch the water drops from our leaky zinc roof. We definitely weren't "eating out of the trash poor", but we *were* poor enough to not have dishwashers, washing machines or dryers. In fact, when I moved to the island we didn't even have a kitchen sink! We washed our clothes by hand and hung them out on a line with clothespins in the backyard to dry. We didn't have hot water so we had to take ice cold showers. Everyone would try to schedule their showers around noon while the sun was high in the sky warming the pipes. At least we had a flushable toilet; my aunt that lived up the hill wasn't as fortunate, she still had an outhouse. We eventually got a two burner stove, but it wasn't big enough to cook a large amount at the same time, so when we had family gatherings we'd still build a big fire in the yard, and cooked outdoors. Ice was a sought after item because we didn't have a freezer. We use to pay Miss West a pretty penny each week for a block of ice to enjoy a cool drink with our Sunday dinners. She was the only one in the neighborhood with a freezer. One pair of shoes would have to last us for years; Luckily my grandfather was a cobbler, so when our shoe soles separated from the actual shoe, he'd meticulously reattach it with his heavy-duty glue. So we were far from homeless and starving but we also didn't have a fraction of the opportunities and luxuries that most Americans take for granted.

LESSON 27: You don't drown in water by falling in it, but by staying submerged.

I'm not saying that you don't have enough reason to be sad; I get it. Some of you are going through some really tough times, but what I am saying is **staying sad isn't going to solve anything**; all it's going to do is attract more sad situations and more sad people to you. If you want to find happiness you have to stop feeling sorry for yourself! If bad things happened to you it's not your fault that you were victimized but it is up to you if you choose to stay a victim.

Don't beat yourself up; all you can give is your best. If you've been giving it your best and you still aren't where you want to be in life, then you have to take some time to reflect and put things in perspective. Don't stress yourself out about where you aren't yet, but reflect on how far you've come. Don't compete and compare yourself to others because each individual measures success differently. You can only be the best version of yourself. Someone else may not have had to overcome the conditioning that you've had to, or perhaps they had a head start because they had supportive parents. Whatever their case may be you'll drive yourself crazy constantly competing and comparing. Half of the time the things in the media are exaggerated and half of the things you read on social media aren't all the way true. You never know what is happening behind closed doors with folks, and you don't always know what they had to do to get what they have or to get where they are today. Some people have the ability to put on a really good facade.

Stop watching things that makes you sad (like the news), because it seeps into your subconscious and certainly affects your mood. Make it a habit to fall asleep to something positive or funny like Americas funniest home videos, stand up comedy or a comedic radio station. Falling asleep in silence is even better than falling asleep to the news.

Make a conscious effort to **do things that make you feel good.** On the days you don't feel like doing them is when you should push yourself to do them the most.

Separate yourself from dysfunction. Life can be hard enough by itself; you don't have to live a life laced with dysfunction. Whether that dysfunction is packaged in the form of foes, friends or even family isn't the point...you have to get it out of your life. Everyday those condescending remarks will eat at you and eventually you'll have nothing left, no confidence, no self-respect and no happiness. You deserve to be happy...any means necessary. Change your phone number; block dysfunctional people from your email and socials sites or move of the house if that will preserve your self-esteem or give you piece of mind.
Make a list of **positive people** you have access to and reach out to one of those people each day. Hopefully you have a teacher, mentor, counselor, pastor or church member you can communicate with daily to keep you in good spirits.

If it's you're job that's robbing you of your happiness then **quit**! Life is too short to do what you don't want to do, especially for a living. You don't have to quit today but start looking into other options today and start planning your getaway; but always try to part ways on good terms because you never know when you'll have to use them for a referral.

Just say "No". It's okay to be little selfish until you get yourself together, because until you take time to build up yourself and get to where you need to be, then you'll be of no use to others. If you're constantly giving but not building, then it will be only a matter of time before you crumble.

Make more money! For many people their bank account correlates with their happiness. It shouldn't be but that's just the way it is for many. If you are one of those people who just don't feel good when you don't have and money, the key is to simply make more money! Take ten minutes now to make a list of 100 things you can do to make more money. It may only be a few dollars here and there but all those dollars add up.

If you've been sad for a while now and just can't seem to shake it or you can't seem to pinpoint anything that's specifically causing you to feel this way, then you may be clinically depressed and need to speak to a professional.

SURVIVOR'S REMORSE

Because a person doesn't express depression the same as most people do, doesn't mean they don't feel it. Some people deal with it differently. For some it shows through promiscuity, alcoholism or by isolation. Others have the ability to hide depression even from those closest to them. For instance, one of my best friends KJ; a gentle man, a lady's man, the life of the party and always wore a smile. After not receiving a response to my text message from him, I logged on to his Facebook page. My jaw dropped, my heart sunk, and tears streamed down my face as I read hundreds of Rest In Peace messages from his friends. He ended his life by jumping off of the roof from his twelve-story penthouse in the middle of downtown LA.

He was a 30-year old bachelor, highly intelligent, spoke four languages, had a great personality, a great paying job, and lived in a pent house in one of the most sought after cities in the world. None of that mattered because he was empty inside. He felt like he had no reason to live and just didn't feel like his life mattered. The news was devastating to me but it wasn't a *shock*. Because two years prior, we had a long heart to heart conversation and he shared with me that one day he went up on his roof and he almost jumped. *He was struggling with some things that happened in his past that he just couldn't seem to get over.* He told me that while he was on the roof looking down at the street below...decided if he should jump or not...he decided to get a puppy. He thought that caring for another life would have given him purpose...and it did...for a while.

KJ and I lived together for a year and he showed no signs of depression during that time. It was around the time I wrote my first book, he helped me edit it, he coached me through my media interviews, he built my website and was the president of my fan club. Looking back, I guess my project and just having someone there gave him purpose...for a while. And then I left. I moved away from LA. We kept in contact but it wasn't as often as it could have been. If I called him more often I would have known that he had given his dog away and that could have indicated that he was headed for a downward spiral. *I know* it wasn't my fault but the questions still haunt me...what if I didn't move? What if I kept in contact more, or what if I told someone else the feelings he shared with me on that one cold night...would he still be alive? I know I tried. I gave him so many suggestions on things he could do to give his life more meaning, like have a child or volunteer for the Boys And Girls Club, but unfortunately nothing I suggested appealed to him.

<u>LESSON 28:</u> People need a purpose to want to live, but each person has to find purpose for themselves.

Sometimes you have to stop thinking about yourself for a moment to see the bigger picture. Do you realize that some people don't even have clean water to drink? Imagine having to choose between dying of dehydration or drinking dirty water that you *know* will make you and your children very, very sick. Well, in some parts of the world that is the biggest decision some mothers are faced with every *single* day. They say: If everyone in the world threw all their problems in one pile and you could exchange your problem for anyone else's, chances are you'd grab yours back in a hurry. So when you start feeling sorry for yourself look at the bigger picture.

On most people's list of things to be happy for, besides health and family, is freedom. But even in prison one can be free. Look at Nelson Mandela! They took his freedom but they couldn't take his spirit. If you're someone reading this from inside those walls, you still have life, you still have a sound mind, you still have memories and you still have your imagination; so that means you still have a choice, a choice to stay positive and be a better person so you can make a positive impact to those who surround you.

Some days when I'm ready to write and I don't want to be disturbed I leave the house, drive *past* my office and go to Starbucks. You'd be surprised at how many times I see the same people in the same chairs. Lonely people who don't have many friends, family members or much of a social life. They'll pretend to read a newspaper and look up at everyone who comes through the door just hoping to spark a conversation. Most of these people are retired and clearly haven't found their purpose in life. Don't let that be you. Try everything until you find what you love. If you already know what makes you happy then continue to do it, then research ways you can make money doing it, then share it with others.

If you **change your perspective,** you can find happiness in the small things; like having a picnic, buying fresh flowers, walking on the beach, reading a book at a park, listening to music, working out, watching the rain, or even biting into your favorite fruit. It doesn't have to be expensive or grand activity to be splendid. Increments of small doses of 'happy" can lead to a lifetime of happiness. It's all about your perspective

LEARN TO ADOPT YOUR OWN VIEWS

In my interviews I've uncovered that a lot of people associate wealth with negative feelings. A lot of people think if someone is rich then he must be a bad person, he must have hustled people out of their money or broke the law or obtained his money immorally. With an outlook like that no wonder most people are having a problem hitting their financial goals. What message are you really sending to yourself if you think in such a way? Consciously or subconsciously if you view rich people as bad...then why would you want to become rich? Why would you want to become *anything* like them? You wouldn't now would you? So many things shape the way we feel about money, including religion, politics, school, our parents, our past and our peers. So the first step is to erase some of the misconceptions and ill feelings you have about money.

We automatically adapt the views of the people we're surrounded by and rarely do we ever make a mindful effort to adopt their own views. Sometimes it's our own parent's parenting style: "Money doesn't grow on trees". How many times have you heard that? When I hear parents tell their kids repressive phrase to their kids I quickly interject "Actually...money is made from paper and paper is made out of trees...so money does grow on trees". It always brings a smile to the kid's face...to the parents, not so much.

Sometimes it's the simple minded who taint our views of wealth: "Rich people are evil, they make their money off of the sweat of the poor". Well, in this day and age, it's the poor who *allow* them to".

Sometimes we spend too much time with people who have low self-esteem. People who wouldn't dare cross invisible barriers or step foot in certain establishments because they think: "That's for the rich folks".

Sometimes people in financial denial surround us. They'll say things like: "Money won't make you happy"...Well...neither will being broke! Or they'll say: "Money isn't everything"... but fail to accept that it may not be everything, but it's right up there with air and water! Money isn't everything, but it sure makes things run a lot smoother when you have it. It offers comfort, gives you more choices, and when you can afford the best doctors it can give you access to the best treatments and possible extend your life.

Sometimes the underachievers who surround us shape our views. They'll say: "I rather be happy than be rich" Why can't you be rich AND be happy? *Now there's a thought!*

Sometimes it's even our interpretation of religious scriptures that stunts our financial growth: "For the Love of money is the root of all kinds of evil..."

(1Timothy 6:10) "If money is so evil why do they ask for it in church every Sunday?" I guess it's all about your "interpretation". But I agree with author Robert Kiyosaki when he recited, "The lack of money is the root of evil" ... because I've seen *more people do more evil because they didn't have money, than those with lots of it.*

THOUGHTS CARRY ENERGY

"Thoughts are delayed actions".

Thoughts are things because thoughts impact how you feel and what you do. Be careful what thoughts you allow to occupy your mind because it's only a matter of time before you start acting out what you're thinking. You have the willpower to switch your thoughts at will. Choose to think big, choose to think positive.

LESSON 29: If you don't have anything good to say then don't say anything at all.

Thoughts are only meant to be heard by *you*. Think of thoughts as God's way of giving you an extra chance to not say something stupid, hurtful or just unnecessary. You get a chance to hear what you want to say in your head...before you choose to say it out loud. Ever met someone who thought out loud all the time and had to end up apologizing...all the time? Don't be one of those people. Think things through before you speak. If you don't know the facts, just hold your tongue. Don't go around offering your opinion to people (especially about themselves) without their permission. And remember that just because something is true does not mean that it has to be talked about. So what you don't like your colleagues suit, as long as there isn't a hole or something physically wrong with it stating your opinion really isn't necessary. It won't make things better, and more than likely will cause friction between you both. Before you start to speak ask yourself "Am I actually making a suggestion or simply venting?" "Will my comment solve something or possibly hurt the situation?"

I know a woman (let's call her Shauna), she was known for making sly comments to just about everyone she spoke to. I must admit that some of the statements she made were hilarious and at times she took the words right out of my mouth because I was thinking the very same thing. However, it hurt her in the long run, just because she said it passively or said it with a smile or slight chuckle at the end didn't make it any better. Her associates soon started separating themselves from her and she just couldn't understand why. She would invite them over for dinner parties and hardly anyone would show, no one would remember her birthday...or so they said and it got to the point when no one wanted to hold a conversation with her besides the casual 'hi and bye'. One day when she came to me complaining about how everyone seemed so distant I told her exactly what she was doing to drive everyone away. At first she denied her behavior and seemed totally oblivious to what I was saying. It's when I pointed out specific examples of how she continually verbally tore down everyone that she came in contact with that she got it.

If you are one of those people who have to get the last word, or who randomly blurts out what comes to mind even though those thoughts may be hurtful to others then make a habit to stop because it's only going hurt you in the long run.

<u>LESSON 30:</u> Learn to let go of bad habits, bad people, debilitating philosophies & beliefs you have on limited facts.

Chapter 4

How to Keep Going When
You Have Nothing Left!

HOW TO KEEP GOING! WHEN YOU HAVE NOTHING LEFT!

"If you could see the size of your blessing that's coming, then you would understand the magnitude of the battle you're fighting"

Ross Perot said, *"Most people give up just when they're about to achieve success. They quit on the one-yard line. They give up at the last minute of the game, one-foot from winning the touchdown"*. Re-read those two sentences again and think back to a time when you gave up on something because it got hard, because you had to make sacrifices, or because the reward didn't come quick enough. Now ask yourself what could have happened if you just held on and just kept pushing forward. What could have happened if you just took another step and then another step? When we are the closest to our goals is when things get the hardest. That's when life starts to really test what you're made of. Right when you think you figured out the last piece of the puzzle you have to start all over again, right when you think you are on the home stretch you find out you have to run another lap, right when you finally got your credit cleaned a bill that you accidentally overlooked pops up on it, right when you finished paying off your car it breaks down, right when you're ready to close on your first home then bank tells you they need something else, right when you get your dream job they find something questionable in your background from years ago, right when you were closing in on one year of sobriety someone offers you a drink, right when you're down to your last few hundred dollars, you're torn between starting that business you always wanted to, or pay your rent to keep a roof over your head.

It's called LIFE and every successful person has been faced with major last minute challenges too; no one is exempt. The difference between the successful and everyone else is that on their road to success while they're carrying their load (whether it be mortgages, car notes or bills) when they reach a wall they don't turn back and say, "I can't go any further, at least I tried". The difference is they MAKE a way! They'll drop their load and use it as a stepping-stone to climb over that wall! There are many people who are successful now who had to file bankruptcy, many who lost their homes and cars, many who found themselves on people's couches and in homeless shelters on their search to becoming a better person. Still, they refused to run back to the complacent comfort of a nine-to-five. Actually a lot of very successful individuals have lost everything they had or hit rock bottom at least once or twice.

"Loss is a prerequisite of success"
-Baje Fletcher

If someone is successful and they've never lost anything, be cautious because chances are that they're in their position by luck and the fall just hasn't come yet. It's the process of losing and regaining again that makes successful people successful. It's the building and rebuilding process that reveals character and strengthens.

Something happens internally when you hit rock bottom. When you're sick and tired of being sick and tired ... it brings out a beast in you, and though it doesn't feel like it at the time, it's reaching *THAT* point that ripens *SOMETHING* in you that's *absolutely* necessary for success. That *SOMETHING* is a blended feeling of disappointment and failure, sadness and anger, mixed with passion...passion for more because you've experienced losing it all...and despised it...and that's what's going to make you get it.

"Champions keep going when they don't have anything left in their tank! That's the difference between the greats"
–Doctor Eric Thomas

MY ULTIMATE SACRIFICE

I was 22 when I made the decision to move from Orlando, Florida to Los Angeles, California. I had a dream to model and act, and if I wanted to give it my best shot, then LA was where I needed to be. My mother died from breast cancer a few years prior, and my fiancé and I had just parted ways; so I felt like there was nothing tying me down to Orlando anymore. Mom died leaving 10 children behind and only had .52 cents to her name. That was our inheritance. She never put any of us through school, never owned a home or a car; in fact, she never even had a driver's license. Her only goal was to make it to age 60 so she could ride the bus for .25 cents instead of $1.

I reached the point where my soul began to die. I knew if I didn't get out of Orlando pretty soon, I was going to end up complacent and hopeless like those I was surrounded by. Everyone I knew was okay with just working a regular job, going home to watch TV, and then going to sleep after that in preparation to do it all over again the next day. Between age 15 and 21 I worked at more than fifteen different places. I cleaned toilets, I bagged groceries, I ran cash registers, I pushed papers, I did customer service, I cold called, I sold alarm systems and I even sold cinnamon glazed nuts at basket ball games. I remember thinking…"This can't be life. This can't be it. There has to be more".

One day that life of mediocrity hit me so hard! I would have rather died than live forty more years in and out of meaningless jobs that I hated. So one day I spoke to my two best friends about moving. They had dreams of moving and getting a new start as well…and so we set a date to move to Los Angeles.

When the day came for us to move. I was so excited. I packed my clothes in my car, and strapped my daughter in her car seat. She was about 7 months old at the time. I called Suzie to see if she was finished packing. She said "Baje…LA is kind of a far drive and we've never been there before. I think we should plan things out more before we go". She totally left me hanging, but even though I was crushed I knew that Michelle was my "ride or die" and she was still in…so all was not lost. I called Michelle to see if she was finished packing her things. She answered the phone only after the third call; I could hear the apprehension in her voice. She said, "Baje, I think we should save up some more money first, because anything can happen. What if the tire blows out, or what if an emergency happens on the road?" I can't believe Michelle was backing out on me at the very last minute. I was more than disappointed; I was devastated and felt totally betrayed. Yes, what they were saying made sense. LA was indeed a 36-hour drive, and yes I only had $500 ($300 of which was for gas). But this was no time for making *sense*. This was time for making *moves!* I couldn't allow their carefully chosen rational and realistic words to sink in because then I too would want to chicken out. All they could see were obstacles, but all I saw were opportunities. I forced myself to keep thinking about the positives. At least I had a car for the journey...and at least I'll have $200 when I get there!

Just when I thought that was the hardest decision of my life...it got harder. My daughter's father came running out of the house pleading with me to leave my daughter behind with him. I knew the emotional effects I had to deal with from not being raised with my mother so leaving my daughter behind didn't even cross my mind. I told him that there was absolutely no way in the world I was going to leave my child behind. A few minutes later his mother came out the house to join the debate...and she wasn't on my team. This was only making my decision harder. In less than an hour great grandma heard what was going on and soon she was on the front lawn trying to talk me into leaving my baby behind. I thought these people were crazy for asking me to leave my child; and they thought that I was crazy for wanting to bring a baby with me on this journey into the unknown. Great grandma asked...well Baje, what are you going to do for money? Where will you work? Who will watch her? What if someone does something to her...she's not even old enough to tell you. I didn't have the answers to any of those questions. I got quieter and quieter as the wheels turned in my head. It was the hardest thing to admit...but they were absolutely right. Though *I* was destined for bigger things...the best place for her (at that time) was with them. Their home was *stable*...and most importantly...it was *safe*. With a heavy heart, a lump in my throat & tears in my eyes...I made the *hardest* decision of my life. I left my baby. *Only a mother who lost or left a child could ever understand the depth of that emptiness.*

To date...that has been *the* biggest sacrifice I've had to make on my pursuit to being successful. Even though I left her with her father and his family, and even though I was able to visit her for a week out of each month...it was still *very* hard. I worried about her forgetting me, I worried about us losing our bond, I worried about the possibility of a custody battle, I worried about what people thought of me, and what people were saying about me. I remember after an argument, a close friend of mine told me that I was a bad mother and asked me what was the difference between a dead-beat dad and myself. That really hurt; but one thing I didn't have to worry about was her safety; and that was *the* most important thing. People would ask, "What kind of mother could leave her baby?" They couldn't understand that I left FOR my baby. I left in order to figure *something* out, to get out of the 9-5 rat race, to give her a better life and show her that she can get anything she wants in this world if she only musters up the courage to go and get it! People would never understand if I ran back empty handed. I had to make it happen! If not, I would feel like a failure, a failure as a mother and as a human being.

Well...fast forward years later...I made it happen! It wasn't an easy journey, but I was able to successfully work as a model and actress for over 6 years! I graced the pages of dozens of magazines, landed TV shows on Bravo, BET, MTV, TRU TV, CW Network & more. I then transitioned into writing books. The first one became a best seller after landing me on some national radio shows and TV shows like Dr. Phil. Besides books, I was able to create other streams of residual income and haven't had to work for anyone in over 6 years!! I spend my days doing absolutely *anything* that I want to do...and nothing that I don't! I can sleep all day; I can lie by the pool, I can travel the world, I can mentor and coach others, I can put on goal setting workshops, I can feed the homeless, I can have breakfast, lunch & dinner with friends...and I do. I can literally choose to spend my time doing whatever I want. And that is freedom at its best!

I know you're wondering ... the answer is *yes!* My daughter *does* live with me now...and has been for the past 5 years. She's a straight-A student in gifted classes, and is a blossoming gymnast! It's truly a blessing to wake up to her everyday. It's a blessing to be able to provide for her, and stay home with her if she isn't feeling well, or pick her up from school early if she gets sick. But first I had to lay the foundation. Thankfully, I chose to do so when she was younger and couldn't remember me being gone. I took a chance, and I thank God every day that it worked out.

I'm not telling you to pack up and leave your child behind. Each of our journeys will be different and will require a different set of tools and unique sacrifices. But I am telling you to be willing to make the sacrifice when you figure out what needs to be done for your specific situation.

HOW MUCH DO YOU BELIEVE IN YOUR DREAM?

Do you believe in your dream enough to give it all you've got? If you have a dream, you have to put all your time, money and all your resources into it until it comes to fruition. It's *your* dream, you can't expect anyone else to see it as clearly as you do, and you can't expect anyone to help you to build it. It would be nice if you find people who are willing to assist you, but you shouldn't *expect* help and you shouldn't wait until help arrives to start the building process. It's your dream; it's your responsibility to bring it to life. There is nothing worse than someone who constantly talks about what they're going to do "someday" but never takes any action. You don't have to have all the pieces of the puzzles figured out yet, but just start! People won't believe in you until they realize how much you believe in yourself and you can only prove that by taking action. I often hear successful people ask "Where was everyone when I needed their help? Now that I've made it, everyone wants to help me with things and give me free stuff"...and that is usually how it works. In the beginning it may just be you, but the longer you stick to it, and the more things start coming together...then people will jump on your bandwagon, until then, just stay focused and keep building.

LESSON 31: It is not about *having* ideas...it is about *making* ideas happen.

Everyone has a dream, but only a small percentage of people actually wake up and start working towards that dream, by putting it on paper and making it a goal and then spend each day working toward that goal. People often say: "I'm waiting until I have extra money or until I have extra time to get started". Newsflash...you will never have the ideal amount of money and there will never be a perfect time to start working on your dream. There will always be an excuse available for you to fall back on; when you have your own place, when you move back with mom so you can save money, once the babies start school, once the kids are off to college, once you get a bonus check ...they are all excuses. If you can't put a pen to paper TODAY and at least start writing down your dream on paper to make it real...you'll probably never get started. Each day you allow to pass without taking action, is like a year further you'll be away from your dream.

LESSON 32: Just because your dream is possible, doesn't mean that it's going to be easy.

Funding your dream, or even staying focused on it will not be easy. There very well may be times when you have to choose to skip a meal so you can purchase something that could possibly take you to the next level. Health issues may arise that you'll have to deal with, or maybe at some point you'll have to cope with the loss of a loved one...that's called life. Take a break if you must but don't quit! So how do you continue pressing forward when you feel like quitting? You find your fuel...that's how!

Grab a pen and piece of paper...right now, and then write down all the reasons why you haven't been able to accomplish your goal yet. Because your parents don't approve, because you had kids too early, because you're a single parent, because you work a lot, because you're in school, because you don't have enough money, because you don't have any help, because you don't know how to get started. How many things were holding you back? Only one thing was holding you back and that's YOU!! So look at that paper one last time, then tear it up then toss it in the trash! Those "reasons" are nothing but "excuses!" and as long as you continue to use those things as a crutch, the longer you'll go nowhere!

I know a mother who used to tell her daughter that she was in top shape and only gained weight when she got pregnant with her. That same mother would often remind her daughter that she would have already had her degree if she didn't get pregnant with her while she was in college and had to drop out. Her daughter was *fourteen* at the time...fourteen!! It doesn't take fourteen years to finish a degree or to drop some baby fat, but for fourteen years she repeatedly blamed her failure on her daughter to make herself feel better. Even more spineless than having excuses for why you can't go after your dreams is pinning those excuses on children who can't fight back.

A DOSE OF TOUGH LOVE

I may sound harsh, but it's only because I'm passionate! I'm passionate about fully living and giving life all I've got. Perhaps it's because I've endured so much tragedy that I can really appreciate my life and my freedom. My parents divorced when I was six, I was sent to Jamaica and went to an all girl boarding school for four years where I couldn't speak louder than a certain volume, I had to eat at a certain time, walk in lines, wear uniforms, go to chapel every night, shared a room with thirty other girls, take two minute showers in ice cold water (where sometimes I'd get surprises through the pipes like slime or the occasional small frog). I fractured my hip when I was a teen that landed me in the hospital for three months. Can you imagine not walking for three whole months? Soon after that I was placed in foster care for medical neglect. The doctors said that my parents took too long to bring me to the hospital, (mostly because my mother was manic depressive and was dealing with her own issues). I spent a few years in foster care and by my 17th birthday I had already bounced between 18 different homes. Soon after I came out the government's care, my mother died from breast cancer. I have ten siblings, two of those siblings battled breast cancer, two were struck by vehicles leaving them disabled, and two were the head and are now living with severe complications. So don't tell me about excuses! I could have used any of those events as a crutch to be mediocre and any of those events could have easily been justified but I CHOOSE to see the good in this world and the good in people. I choose to see life as a realm of possibilities, I choose to create big dreams and go after them all. I could be bitter about my past or I could paint an amazing future in spite of it. I refuse to allow anything or anyone to rob me of my positive outlook on life.

I find it hard to sympathize with under-achievers who are blessed with life and freedom but choose to play it safe and fly under the radar; Never taking risks and refusing to give life all they've got. Or the ones whose talent is obvious to everyone around them but they lack the courage to step out on faith and cultivate their talent so they can capitalize off of it or simply share it with the world. It's like a slap in God's face. The only people I sympathize with are those with disabilities, and are mentally or physically unable to reach for their dreams; but even then we hear stories of people with disabilities who defy the odds and find a way. My brother Tony for example, is one of the siblings I mentioned that was shot in the head...he was shot twice...at point blank range. Though that was about twenty-five years ago, he still lives with the consequences today. He has to eat healthy, exercise daily, and take medication three times a day so he doesn't have seizures. He has to have a home-health-aid come to his house to assist him everyday with things we take for granted like cooking. He also lost most of his feeling in one side of his body, so that side is a bit slower than the other. With all those disadvantages he could easily stay home all day and collect public assistance, and it would totally be justified. If he accepted those "limitations" as disadvantages he would have thrown in the towel a long time ago. Instead he dedicated months out of his life to write a book about his life story and the lessons he learned that he wants to pass on. He is also currently in school pursuing his GED even though he doesn't have to. Even though he doesn't have to he slowly gets dressed each day, puts his heavy books in his book bag and goes to school in rain or shine in New York's freezing weather. When I think about him and other people struggling with disabilities, I have no choice but to give my dream every ounce of energy I have, because they would give anything to just have a fair shot.

"I owe society my best shot".
– Baje Fletcher

LESSON 33: Success begins when you eliminate excuses from your reality.

So you don't make enough money? Start doing something that will pay you more! There aren't enough hours in each day? Set your alarm for you to wake up an hour earlier! You're a single mom? Partner up with other single mothers and form a support group! Stop making excuses and start making a way!

FIND YOUR FUEL

Perhaps your dream is already clear to you, but if it isn't, then take a few minutes and allow yourself to daydream. (Stop reading or listening and just daydream for five minutes. It's very important that when I ask you to reflect or do an exercise in this book you do so right away. In order for this book to work, you can't just *read* it; you have to *apply* it as well. The best time to start applying is right now while you're in the moment and before you get distracted with *life*). So close your eyes and answer this question, "If you weren't limited by anything, if you didn't have to work just to pay bills, if you already had all the tools and resources you needed, and if you weren't afraid to fail…then what is it that you would want to do with your life? Why would you want to do that thing in particular? If you accomplish that thing how would it make you feel? If you had to live the rest of your life without ever reaching that goal how would *that* make you feel? Now get a sheet of paper and write down your answers. For example:

If I weren't afraid to fail I would open up my own hair salon.

I'd want to open it up because I love doing hair and I'm great at it and as a teen I used to always do my mother's hair and she always encouraged me to run own my salon one day.

If I opened up my own salon it would make me feel free knowing that I can make my own hours and don't have to be tied down to a nine-to-five. It would also make me proud knowing that I have a business I can pass down to my children.

If I had to live the rest of my life not being able to reach that goal, I'd feel like a failure.

It's important that in this exercise you speak the truth. You can tear up the paper after but it's critical that you get the truth out. It may make you feel uncomfortable to face it or even embarrassed but sometimes those are the emotions that we need to confront in order to make drastic changes.

WHAT IS THERE TO GAIN BY QUITTING?

"Nothing will pay off like persistence."

There will be days when your dream seems so out of reach, there will be days when life beats you down emotionally, physically and spiritually, and there will be days when you'll feel absolutely drained ...and still that's no reason to quit. Take a short break for your sanity but keep moving forward. When you're going through the trials it will feel like forever, you may feel like you're spinning your wheels but getting nowhere, your end vision may seem hazy but keep moving forward. Is there a chance that you may give it all you've got and you never reach your goal? Sure there is that possibility. I can't give you a guarantee on that, but I can absolutely guarantee you that if you quit, you will NEVER reach that goal. What do you have to lose by trying? You're going to spend your time on this earth doing one thing or the other, so you might as well spend it chasing your dream!

Other motivational speakers call it your "why," I call it your "fuel". What is going to fuel you on the days when you feel like giving up? What or who is the reason why you won't quit? There are a few different things that fuel me. I think about my disabled siblings and think about if one day I have to be their caretaker full time I better be able to afford it. I think about how my mother died with nothing to leave any of her ten children and I didn't want to be that mom. I think about my father who is about to retire, and even though he is healthy now he may not be as strong in ten or twenty years and I need to be able to take care of him financially so he doesn't end up in some rundown nursing home. I think about the women who write in to me daily telling me that I'm an inspiration to them and I want to continue to inspire them. Most of all I think about my daughter who looks up to me and who will one day aspire to be all that I am, so I must set the bar high! So when *you* feel like quitting think about *your fuel*...and get that fire back blazing! Print a photo of what fuels you, write a sentence about what fuels you or draw a representation of it and bring it with you in your wallet all the time...and the days when you feel drained and confused and frustrated and it seems like things are falling apart or you're drifting further and further from your dreams...pull it out and look at it.

PREPARE FOR THE THINGS YOU CAN'T PREVENT

No one escapes life untouched, we all will have battles we'll have to face. The key is to have a backup plan! Ask yourself what bad things could possibly happen that would totally throw you off of your game, and then prepare *prior* to the misfortune. This doesn't mean to dwell on it or even expect it, but make preparations just in case. Prepare *before* losing a loved one, getting robbed, getting fired, getting depressed, getting sick or having a break down. And just by asking yourself how you can be prepared and then taking action, you'll actually be *preventing* some of those occurrences.

Financial preparation can be in the form of learning about money, starting a savings account with an emergency fund, investing, having a retirement account, having multiple streams of income, having a will, having a power of attorney, getting out of debt, monitoring your credit, guarding yourself against identity fraud, insuring your assets, or getting life, health, disability and unemployment insurance.

Physical preparation can be getting a home alarm system, getting a watch dog, taking a self defense class, getting a concealed weapon permit, exercising often, taking daily vitamins, drinking plenty of water, eating healthy, and getting routine check ups.

Mental preparation can be reading books, seeking mentors, habitually studying material in your field and playing mental games that stimulate your mind (like those on lumosity.com),

Emotional preparation can be meditating, doing yoga and getting relaxing massages.

Spiritual preparation can be spending time with positive friends and family members, talking to a pastor (or other spiritual leader), speaking with a life coach, mentor or psychologist, watch or read materials on spirituality, and praying.

THE HAPPY FILES

Have a list of things that make you feel good and that motivate you on hand. So on the days that you are down you know exactly what will pick you up. For example:

Keep busy,
Go to the spa,
Go to the gym,
Get my nails done,
Do my hair & makeup,
Listen to my upbeat playlist,
Have a glass of my favorite wine,
Volunteer for those less fortunate,
Meet with my two favorite girl friends,
Watch America's Funniest Home Videos,
Get my favorite dessert from my local bakery,
Watch some motivational videos on YouTube,
Do something on the side to make extra money,
Visit someone's social site who only post positive or funny things.

When calamity hits, you won't know up from down. The times when you need positivity, motivation, encouragement, or reinforcement the most, will be the times when it's hardest to stay on track, so by having your "Happy Files" already prepared you should be able to get back on track much faster.

THE QUEST TO SUCCESS

Pursuing your dream will not be easy. If success were effortless then everyone would experience it. It's going to take taming your ego, swallowing your pride, strategizing, recognizing opportunities, taking calculated risks, making sacrifices, being persistent, having patience, and most of all...being disciplined! The most common problem faced by those on the journey of self improvement isn't that they don't know what they need to do, it's the fact that they are not disciplined enough to do it.

CULTIVATING DISCIPLINE

LESSON 34: The difference between a goal and an accomplishment is discipline.

It won't happen overnight. It will take months and years to master each area that you want to be disciplined in, but you can do it if you stay focused. Whether it's eating healthier, exercising daily, saving more money, waking up earlier or controlling your temper, it all starts with a *decision*. You have to make up your mind and make a commitment to yourself that you are going to give 100%. Don't overwhelm yourself with a lot sudden changes, to increase your chances of success only take on one big habit that you want to change every three months or so. Once you start tackling the area of your choice don't get discouraged if those around you don't notice some improvement right away. Your progress may be slow...but it's *progress*.

"People get paid in public for what they practice in private"

PERSISTENCE & PATIENCE, & THE LINE IN BETWEEN

There is a line between being determined and being flat out annoying. How thick or thin that border is really depends on the individual you're dealing with. Some people have a high tolerance for these things than others. No matter who you're dealing with, never take the first NO for a final answer. Never ask when they have free time. No successful person ever has "free time", you have to pick a time on a weekday between nine and five and just call them. (Try to avoid Mondays though, usually Mondays are hectic". Don't text and ask, "When is a good time to call", just call and ask "Can you spare five minutes", or "Do you have a few minutes to chat right now?" If they don't, then they'll let you know when is a good time to call. People can tell when you are afraid of them, or when you feel like you're not worth their time and they may start treating you like that if they pick up on that insecurity. Think about it...if you don't feel like you are worth their time, why should they give it to you?

WHAT'S YOUR REASON WHY?

Figuring out the real reason why you really want to be successful will give you your best shot at it. What's going to keep you on track and keep you excited to get out of bed, work long hours, workout everyday, cold call potential customers, save more money, or get out of debt. Figure out *why* you can't give up, why you can't put things on hold, why you HAVE TO find a way through every hurdle you'll face.

Once you set a goal ask yourself why are you working towards it? If the reason isn't significant enough then chances are you will not succeed at it. Ask yourself what is at stake if you aren't able to accomplish this goal? What will you lose if you do not succeed? Perhaps it's your reputation, your lifestyle or your pride.

Remind yourself of all the sacrifices you had to make just to get where you are today, remind yourself of the obstacles you've overcome so far and the pain you've already endured; don't let it be in vain. You didn't come all this way for nothing! Remind yourself of all the people who are waiting for you to fail just so they can say: "I told you so" and don't give them the satisfaction of tasting those words. This is your chance to prove them wrong! Think of those who you will let down if you don't succeed, your children, your parents, or your partner.

Now ask yourself what do you deserve. Do you deserve a life of strife and struggle? Do you want be trapped in the rat race until you're sixty? Or do you desire a stress-free life of abundance. Personally…I don't think that we were put on earth to just work then wait to die. I don't think we're here just to work to pay bills either. I don't think we were created to spend the best years of our lives for someone else and just to help others build their dreams while ours wither by the wayside. What sense does it make…to slave away while we are in our prime, what sense does it make to squander our youth working just to retire when the best years of our lives are over…Does that make sense to you?

I'm glad I saw the light at an early age. It's been ten years so far since I've had to clock into a job and I'm hoping after you finish this book and apply the lessons you'll be able to start experiencing some of the freedom that I have been. The key is to have multiple streams of residual income and to have business systems in place that will make money even when you aren't present.

Think of all the opportunities that you already missed. Think of all the times when you said: "I wish I had", "I should have", "I could have"...today is your chance to start over!

THE ENABLED

The problem with some people is that they have a crutch (something or someone to fall back on when times get rough). Those crutches can come in the form of an inheritance, a spouse, or parents who enable "bumish" behavior! Some people can always run back home to mama when they get fired, or quit or just get lazy. They know that as long as mama is alive they'll always have a clean bed and a hot meal waiting. People ask me all the time...why am I so driven? Why do I not take no for an answer and how do I happily take risk after risk? My answer is "because I have to". I've been on my own since I was 17. I don't have a mother to run back to "if things don't work out," I don't have the luxury of having a plan B. And for most people they'll never realize their full potential until they don't have a backup plan and it's do or die.

THE INVISIBLE

The next set of people who can't seem to get it together are the ones who don't have anyone who depend on them. No children, no family, no partner and no friends. They've never accomplished *anything* of *any* significance so they have nothing at stake if they lose. They feel invisible, unwanted, and just don't think they matter. No one expects greatness from them, so they don't expect greatness from themselves.

If you are one of those people I want to let you know that you matter. You matter! You wouldn't have been created if you did not matter. I don't care if your mom said you were an accident, it's not up to her. It was up to GOD and each and every one of us who made it here has a purpose. I use the phrase "made it", because I don't believe that any of us are here by chance. Fertility clinics are full of couples who can't get pregnant and thousands of women who are pregnant have miscarriages everyday. Many women bring their babies to the ninth month just to realize the child is stillborn and many babies are born without limbs, with incurable diseases or with extensive and irreversible brain defects. It is no mistake that you are here AND in sound mind. Be grateful...be great!

Don't dwell on it if you don't have anyone to grind for, or anyone who you can make proud...you don't need permission from anyone to be great, be great for you. The irony in this is once you start treating yourself like you matter then others will do the same.

BRING YOUR STOCKS UP

<u>LESSON 35</u>: Anything that can be obtained easily can also be taken away just as easily.

Too many people want something for nothing. Instead of seeking things of value without having to put out much time or effort try increasing your self worth or self value...or as I like to say: "bring your stocks up". Increase your mental value, physical value, financial value, social value. There are a lot of ways you can build value. You can build value by getting educated.

<u>Mental Value:</u> Everyone doesn't have high self-esteem. How we feel about ourselves often stretches back to childhood, how we were raised and more importantly by whom we were raised. If we were lucky we were surrounded with love and people who built us up, but unfortunately that isn't always the case. Some of us were raised in households that lacked a parent, or both parents. Some of us lost our parents at a young age, or didn't get the time or affection we individually

deserved because there were a lot of siblings in the house or because of income restrictions or our parents had to work overtime. For those of us, we have to learn how to build our own self-esteem. Some confidence boosting exercises include:

Repeating affirmations daily. Which is speaking how you want to feel or how you want to see yourself into existence. For example, I am outgoing, hard working, beautiful and I deserve the best out of life. Be as specific as possible and tailor your affirmation to fit you.

Watching motivational videos on the Internet. It can be of a motivational speaker giving a speech, or an interview of someone that you admire. For instance, I often look up videos of Tyler Perry, Will Smith, Tyrese Gibson, Les Brown, Eric Thomas & Oprah. Those people inspire me because they all came from a background where their future looked dim to bystanders, but they were able to see *beyond* their current circumstances and they also had the courage to breathe breath into the life that they (and they alone) envisioned in their minds. Another video that inspires me is a four-minute clip of Beyoncé singing "I was here" at the United Nations building for 'world humanitarian day'. I found it on YouTube and I try to watch it every morning to remind myself that the world is so much bigger than what I think and that there are still millions of people out there who need help and it serves as a reminder that I must do my part. To make this world a better place than I found it.

Listen to audio CD's or music that make you feel good. Perhaps it's songs that remind you of great childhood memories, or songs that put you in an energized state of mind to make you want to go out and do great things.

Instead of watching mindless television watch something motivational or inspirational like the OWN network. Or perhaps watching an episode of "The lives of the Rich and Famous" will open your appetite for a luxurious lifestyle.

Read biographies of people you admire. In case you don't like to read books or can't find the time to, then consider reading magazines (they're shorter and usually get straight to the point). You can also read online articles or read bios of those people on Wikipedia.com

<u>Physical Value:</u> Take care of your body from the inside out. Exercise. Losing weight is one of the hardest goals to accomplish for most people. It's one of the hardest because we live in the 'microwave age', we live in a time where we want everything instantly and because we don't see instant results we often get

discouraged. I recommend using 'mile markers' and workout partners. Drink plenty of water, take vitamins daily, eat healthy, exercise everyday and get plenty of sleep.

<u>Financial Value</u>: Read books on credit building, mortgages, taxes, saving, budgeting, investing, compound interest, retirement plans, insurance (auto, life, disability, unemployment, homeowners etc.) Get a good accountant and financial advisor; accountants look behind and financial advisors look ahead).

<u>Social Value:</u> Place yourself in the right circles. Constantly network and build strong & profitable business and social connections. When your name is brought up in a conversation what do people say about you? What do you have a reputation for? Your word should be your bond. You must make it a habit of doing what you say you are going to do and you must not make promises that you can't keep.

REPUTATION IS EVERYTHING

"Reputation is everything, guard it with your life".

What's the difference between not caring what other people think and guarding your reputation? The difference is you should never allow what someone thinks about you, or what someone says about you, so much that it hinders you from going after your dreams. The fact is people are always going to talk. They will always have an opinion no matter what you do, but you can't allow their outlook on life to hinder how you want to live. At the same time, do what you can to keep your name out the mud because once it is tarnished it can't always be untainted. Don't put yourself in questionable situations. Don't hang out at seedy places and don't associate with shady people. Only associate with those who speak highly of others to you, because chances are they'll speak highly of you to others as well.

CLOAK OF CHARACTER

So fast-forward to today...how can someone with my kind of personality go on to model in magazines, act on TV, and be a motivational speaker? It was because I *consciously chose* to. When it's time for me to meet people for the first time, do business with new clients or speak to a room full of people and I'm nervous, I give myself a pep talk. Call it weird...but whatever works. I think about someone who I look up to and I ask myself how would they act in this situation, and then I act accordingly. I remind myself that people are just people so there is no need to be afraid of them. Most importantly I think about what I have to lose if I don't land that gig, or ace that interview or wow those potential clients; then I go in there and kill it! The more I *acted* as if I wasn't nervous, the more I realized that people could not tell that I was nervous, so I just continued to play it off and surprisingly it got easier and easier to just be myself...the real me...under all the shyness.

In fact, many public figures are a lot more reserved and withdrawn from their public persona but when it's time to be "on"...they turn on. The Huffington Post reports that Courteney Cox, Christina Aguilera, former first lady Laura Bush, and even BILLIONAIRES Bill Gates and Warren Buffet are all introverts. Beyoncé is also an introvert and that's why she created the persona

"Sasha Fierce". Many entertainers, performers and people in the public eye put on a "cloak of character" or create "alter egos" in order to get out of their shell.

"Roman is my alter ego...He says things I can't say". —Nicki Minaj

Naturally I'm an introvert. I'm reserved, soft spoken and like to sense my surroundings and read people before I start opening up. But the funny thing is, it was easier...in fact thrilling for me to get dressed up and take photos, walk the runway or be on stage. I had the chance to act like someone else for a few hours and in those hours there was no pressure of acceptance; I felt free from judgment and scrutiny of others because after all I was "in character".

Shy people aren't noticed, shy people aren't remembered and as a result shy people have a hard time getting what they want. In your personal life it's not so much of a hindrance but in business it's detrimental. The great news is that it is something that you can get over if you really want to. You have to learn how to interact with people in a way where they aren't uncomfortable because you are uncomfortable. The more you make an effort to break out of your shell the easier it gets. When you walk into a room of strangers don't be afraid to be the first one to greet them, or introduce yourself or extend your hand for a handshake. You never know what doors those strangers can open for you in the future by simply saying something to break the ice...like "hello". You can tell a joke, or tell them about something that you've recently seen in the news or simply give them a sincere compliment on their shoes, hat or hairstyle or just ask a question.

USE THE NON-BELIEVERS

Instead of letting the non-believers *stop* you, use them to them *fuel* you. Let the words they spew light a fire under you as if it's gasoline. There are two types of people in this world; One hears "You can't" and they stop trying, but the other hears "You can't" and responds with "You just wait and see!"...I'm the latter; which one are you?

LESSON 36: Don't let others judge you off of their capacity.

For instance, when I first told people I was writing my first book they gave me the 'yeah right' look but that didn't deter me. A lot of people doubted me but the only thing I could have done at that point was prove them wrong. I remember being interviewed on a radio show and telling the interviewer that I had plans to write my first book. He asked, "So which publisher is going to publish it?" I said, "Actually, I'm going to self-publish it". He started laughing then said, "That book won't make it past the copier machine at Kinkos". There was a moment of silence, and then his colleagues starting laughing as well. Did it hurt my feelings? Absolutely! Did it stop me? Absolutely not!!

I finished writing my book, and then I got the cover designed. I printed out the cover and wrapped it around a book that I was reading at the time. I bought it everywhere with me. I used that mock copy to promote my book even before it was published. I told everyone about it, I brought it to every event I attended and I asked every influential person I met to take a photo with it some politely declined and some supported me (including Paris Hilton, Hugh Heffner, Cynthia Bailey of Atlanta Housewives, rappers E 40 and Waka Flocka, & also best selling author Robert Kiyosaki). I remember going into a bookstore and placing the copy of my mock book on the shelves beside the other books...then I stepped back and took a photo of it. At that very moment I *promised* myself that I wasn't going to stop until my book was published and in bookstores. I had a point to prove...to that radio station and everyone else who doubted me. For the following months I worked day and night to publish it and promote it. Fast forward a year later and after many shut doors, phone calls and emails, I not only made it on Dr. Phil, TRU TV's "In Session", The Big Tigger Morning Show, Frank Ski Morning Show and The Breakfast Club...but I also got a letter from Barnes and Nobles bookstore saying they would like to place and initial order for my books nationwide. *I never break a promise...especially to myself.*

TALENT vs. TENACITY

Persistence, determination, perseverance, strength of purpose, tirelessness, patience, purposefulness.

te·nac·i·ty
1 The quality or fact of being able to grip something firmly; grip."

Your talent may open doors for you but it's your tenacity that will keep those doors open once you walk though. A good friend of mine often uses the quote: *"Hard work beats talent when talent doesn't work hard'.* Many times I've seen a person who isn't super talented, overly gifted or highly intelligent but gets the position they're competing for because of their tireless work ethic.

"Often times it's not the most talented person that gets what they want but the most persistent".

One YouTube video that I watch repeatedly to stay motivated is one about Will Smith. He said that he may not be the most talented but he is *the* hardest working. When his competition sleeps, he trains, when his competitors rests he practices. I remember him saying that if you put him on a treadmill to run against someone else, only one of two things is going to happen: he will outrun the other person or he will die on that treadmill! Quitting is absolutely not an option for him. Now…that's dedication.

<u>LESSON 37:</u> The only way you'll know for sure that something will not work out is if you quit, so never quit!

I don't stop until I get what I want regardless of the consequences, sacrifices and how long it will take. I've been that way since I was a child. My aunt Willet who raised me realized that quality in me at a young age. As a child, I'd often hear my name in the same sentences with words like stubborn, hard headed, and defiant whenever my elders would speak of me or to me, because even if the thing I wanted wasn't in my best interest there still would be no stopping me; No long talk, no punishment and no spanking. Today my colleagues use words like persistent and determined to describe me. Do I think that's a coincidence? Not by a long shot. The biggest change in me was my choices...I chose to go after things that would better me, rather than things that would hinder me in life. Some of us are naturally born with a tenacious spirit (but we get it talked out of us or even spanked out of us growing up)...and for some of us, it's a skill that we have to absorb. Often, it's the same traits that get us in trouble in school and at home as children, are the same exact traits that will get us ahead in the business world once we are adults; isn't that comical? But we all are capable of narrowing in and locking down on a goal with the grip of a pit bull's jaw. The key is finding your fuel and being able to mentally tap into that source whenever the occasion calls for it.

"Most people give up just when they're about to achieve success. They quit on the one-yard line. They give up at the last minute of the game one foot from a winning touchdown."
– Ross Perot

PAY YOUR DUES

<u>LESSON 38:</u> If success were easy, everyone would succeed.

Becoming successful will not be easy, but it *will* be worth it in the end. Sometimes you'll have to do things that make you very uncomfortable; that's called "paying your dues". When you do those things, do them without complaining and find comfort in knowing that it is apart of the *success process*. Know that every single person who is successful, had to do some things that they did not want to do in order to get where they wanted to go. It's a little give and take. They had to put in long hours, they had to do years of research, they had to take jobs that they didn't particularly like and they had to work with people who they could not stand, and do it all while wearing a smile. Each hurdle you jump over will take you closer to your goal of buying a home, starting your business or retiring early. Whatever your goal is keep your eye on the prize and don't dwell on the sacrifice. Think of it as a trade-off. If you have a financial goal to meet, you may not be able to go out with your friends for happy hour everyday, or party with them every weekend. You have to be okay with that in order to thrive financially in the long run. Even better, find some friends with similar goals to yours; working on your goals together will lessen the feeling of missing out.

"Live like no one else, so later you can live like no one else" – Dave Ramsey

ONE HIT WONDERS

You may have heard of a singer who wrote just one song and instantly found worldwide success, or so it seems. We may never know how long they've been writing, how many people turned them down or how many songs they wrote that *never* made it. We often don't get to see their struggles, financial losses, amount of rehearsals & setbacks. To us looking in from the outside it seems so easy but it isn't…and for the few who find fame & fortune, or are put in a power position with very little effort, they don't stay in that position for very long because there was no mental preparation. A wind of luck may have swept them in the right direction, but preparation is the root that will keep them grounded. That's why most people who win the lotto end up bankrupt in just a matter of a few years; that's why there are a lot of 'one hit wonders' in the music business, and that's why politicians who weren't meant for the position in the first place won't get reelected for a second term… We all must pay our dues.

"Opportunity favors the prepared mind".

THE ART OF NEGOTIATING

LESSON 39: Never take the first NO for a final answer.

Once you hear the first NO that means that the negotiating process has just begun.

NO = Manager. Once you hear the second NO, ask for their manager, they'll try to deter you by telling you that the manager will tell you the same thing. Act as if you didn't even hear that comment and ask for the manager again. Even if you were a bit irritated with the first representative don't let that tone transfer to the manager. Be super cordial and explain the situation...not emotionally but logically. Point out specific scenarios, use exact days and times, refer to previous people you spoke to by name.
Your Best shot. One you speak to a decision maker and they tell you what they are willing or AREN'T willing to do to accommodate you, don't hastily accept the first offer. Even if it's a great deal, ask, "Is that the best you can do?"...Then wait.

Is That All You've Got? Understand that not every item can be discounted but ask what else can you get instead. Perhaps they're able to throw in something else for free, or give you a discount on something else.

Silence Is Golden. Don't speak too much because you don't want to *oversell* your situation. Say what you have to say matter-of-factly and then let them fill the awkward silence.

Start Low. When negotiating for something you're buying, then start out at half of what you actually want to pay for the item. Half may seem like a relatively low offer but it will give you more room to negotiate.

Double Up. When negotiating for money, pay, or items that have a monetary value, always ask for more than what you need...preferably double. Because more than likely the other person is going to talk you down if they're accustomed to negotiating, and when they do hopefully they'll meet you in the middle, which is all you wanted in the first place.

But Why? If you have valid and specific reasons why they should pay more or why you should pay less, now is the time to fire away.

Thanks But No Thanks. If it's a business that has a big call center don't be afraid to say "Thank You", disconnect the call and call back a few more times until you get a hold of a representative who will accommodate your request.

Patience Is A Virtue. The person who has the most patience will have the upper hand. So never walk into a negotiation when you're feeling desperate. (Actually the best time to negotiate for something is *before* you actually need it).

The Walk of Pride. If they're not willing to meet your terms and it's a business you have an account with of use frequently, ask them if they'd rather you do business elsewhere? In the rare event they say yes, then be willing to walk away and find a better deal elsewhere. Same thing applies to a job where you're not getting paid what you're worth.

Sometimes Losing Is Actually Winning. Have the courage to walk away if the deal isn't right. In most negotiations, it's when one party is about to walk away that the other party gives in. But in the event that doesn't happen, then be strong enough to keep it moving. (Just leave your contact info with them in case they change their mind later on).

Win Win. The best deals negotiated are ones where both parties are happy, otherwise the deal won't be permanent or you won't be able to work together in the future, so it's best to find some common ground if you both can.

LESSON 40: In negotiating, the best defense is preparation, so know what you want.

I have never met a successful person in business who was afraid to negotiate; whether it's business deals, settlements, contracts or salary, they have all mastered the art.

When at all possible, don't buy off impulse. If you can, go to the store and look at the things that you want *before* the day that you are prepared to buy them. That way the rush from the new item has worn off and you can actually make a logical decision.

Remember anything is negotiable if you talk to the right decision maker. So before you start negotiating make sure that the person you are about to negotiate with has the power to reduce the price.

Know your bottom line. Know ahead of time what you want out of the deal, and what you are or aren't willing to settle for.

Always see what kind of deal the other person is willing to give you first. Because you may shout out an opening bid and it may be lower that what they were going to offer you.

Start the negotiation by asking for *more* than what you want, because if someone is well versed in the art or negotiating then chances are they are going to try and talk you down or ask for some sort of a discount. (If they happen not to, then you can still knock something off the price and they'll be happy to get that discount).

When it's time to shop for bargains, don't dress like you have a lot of money, but when it's time to sell...then dress like you do. Because it's hard to get a discount on anything if it looks like you can afford it.

The best negotiators leave everyone in a win/win situation. A successful negotiation should only end when both parties are mutually satisfied. There is no victory in winning one single negotiation...but never being able to do business with that person again because they feel low-balled.

THE ART OF PERSUASION

<u>LESSON 41:</u> Persuasion is making people WANT to do what you want them to do.

People who are great at persuading others don't rely on luck. There is an art to getting people to do what you want *willingly*, and them not regretting it later. Great persuaders usually have a few of the following traits in common.

They communicate effectively. They know what they're talking about, what they want and how to relay their message. You'll never be able to get what you want if you're incapable of conveying your needs.

They speak with body language. They realize that verbal communication is secondary, and that your body speaks long before you do; they not only pay attention to what it is saying but they subtly mimic your style of body talk. Not only the volume or tone of your voice, the way you speak with your hands, but even the way you sit.

They smile genuinely. Nothing breaks the ice than an authentic smile...and nothing is more transparent than a fake one.

They turn on the charm. They lead with charisma; and though not everyone is born charismatic, it's definitely a skill that can be learned and summoned at will. It's like a tango with a friendly flirt, so subtle that one could do it in front of their partner and it wouldn't be crossing boundaries.

They have a strong presence. It's that "something", that "star-power" that most can't explain in just one sentence, but everyone indisputably recognizes it. It's often a combination of things. It may start with immaculate posture, the way they walk, the way they speak with authority all while possessing a smile that lights up any room.

They exude power. Not power in the sense of the overbearing type, but an authentic sheath of self-confidence.

They are warm and inviting. It's hard to persuade anyone to do anything *willingly* if you are intimidating, cold or unenthusiastic.

They build personal rapport. They find commonalities between themselves and others and talk about those similarities before they start talking business. It may be something as small as quickly scanning the room for photos, souvenirs or degrees; perhaps they both have children the same age, both traveled to the same places or even went to the same schools. They understand that anything in common helps at breaking the ice.

They make you feel good about yourself. This can be with a small but sincere compliment on your hair, choice of clothes or even taste in music.

They make it all about you, not themselves. They make you feel important by asking you questions about your interests and things you care about. And you'll find that they actually listened because they can recite what you said. Even if they don't agree with what is being said, they allow the other person to finish what they're saying and never cut them off. They are patient enough to wait to say their piece.

<u>LESSON 42:</u> After speaking to a great salesman, he will make you feel like he is the most interesting person in the world, but after speaking to a great persuader he will make you feel like YOU are the most interesting person in the world.

They show they care. This may be done by taking time to hear you out or by making eye contact and giving you their undivided attention.

When they're persuading others to buy **they give choices** so everyone one feel likes it a win-win situation. However there has to be a sense of scarcity as well. They can't feel like your offer will be on the table indefinitely or they'll be in no rush to take action. You have to give them a deadline.

They allow others to speak on their behalf. They understand that a third party recommendation goes a longer way than tooting their own horn. This third party can be an employee or just a friend.

They share their favorable reviews. They realize that people want what other people want so they reintegrate to new prospects what others have said about the positive impact that their products or services have made.

They humbly lead with their accomplishments. They know the importance of having a strong and dependable brand so they utilize their titles, credentials and awards to strengthen their positioning.

They're detail oriented. They not only point out benefits, but unique selling points and what prospects can lose if they don't try their product or service.

They pay attention to the words you use and how you use them because those are cues to what type of person you are, what you want and how you operate. Do you have a passive personality and use words like remember, could, maybe, feel. Or are you the more assertive type and use words like, should, definitely and think? They know words are reflections of personality traits and they utilize that information in their pitches.

They know the power of touch. A light tap on the shoulder may break the ice, a simple handshake or hug may seal a deal. Getting a prospect to simply try, touch or hold a sample of your product may be the difference between losing or landing that client. By having a potential client physically writing in her own name in your appointment book may be the difference between her keeping or breaking that scheduled appointment.

They give before they expect to receive. The token can be small but it is usually thoughtful, unexpected or personalized. It can also come in the form of a favor. It's hard for most people to say no to someone when that person has done something considerate for them in the past.

Chapter 5

Hard Work Vs. Smart Work

HARD WORK Vs. SMART WORK

LESSON 43: To work hard use your muscles, but to work smart...use your mind.

Many people spend most of their lives working HARD to make someone else's dream a reality. Are you one of them? Do you play by the rules, do all that you're asked to do, are the first one on the job and the last one to leave but it seems like you're still not getting ahead? I've seen too many people slave away at jobs for decades, and still are in the same position; or are only making just a few dollars more per hour more than when they started. Even though they've worked the hardest they're still far from where they want to be. Two people can put in the same amount of hours working but one can be way ahead because of *how* they worked. Working smart is about being effective and efficient.

"It is not enough to be busy... The question is: what are we busy about?"

- Henry David Thoreau

THE 40-YEAR TREADMILL

It doesn't matter how hard you work or how long you work if you're not working in the right way or not working on the things that will not get you ahead. How many hard workers do you know that are in the same place for 5, 10 or 20 years? Odds are *many!* Most people think that they're winning if they get a raise for a few dollars or even few thousand dollars every year, but the truth is they aren't. Between inflation, rising cost of living and simultaneously increasing their lifestyle they're stuck exchanging their time for money. Most people don't realize that it's not necessarily *hard work* that gets them ahead, but it's *smart work* that does.

"Working hard alone only makes you tired, working smart is what gets you ahead".

Sadly our society is designed to propel people who work with their minds, all while the muscle of this country, (the people who literally work hard with their hands run on "the 40 year treadmill"). What's even sadder is that these hardworking law-abiding citizens run so hard that they never have a chance to look up to even question the system. So in a society that caters to the rich and with a growing gap between the "haves and the have-nots" how do you get ahead? You learn from the rich...that's how!

<u>LESSON 44:</u> Just because you are "busy", doesn't mean that you are productive. So get busy doing the right things.

FIND A MILLIONAIRE MENTOR

You can start by seeking millionaire mentors. I understand that you may not have access to them directly, but you may have access to someone who knows them well, someone who works for them or someone who has learned a lot from them. You can go to a seminar or workshop that they're conducting. You can go to the library and borrow their autobiography or any other books they may have written in order to get some insight on how they think or how they operate. You can go in a bookstore and read articles about them in magazines or you can simply read or watch every interview they ever done for free on the Internet. Your mentors don't always have to be millionaires. Look around for successful people in your city, go to events where they'll be attending and businesses that they own and make the introduction. It may sound a little mechanical if you flat out ask, "Can you be my mentor?" but just tell them that you admire what they do and they seem like someone you'd be able to learn quite a bit from and is it ok for you to call them with some questions that you may have from time to time.

BE SMART

The number one lesson in working smart is not working for money but making money work for you. All of chapter 8 is dedicated to money. Other examples of "smart work" are sprinkled all throughout this book. It's intertwined in tasks such as managing your time, managing your money, being disciplined, being prepared, prioritizing, and taking calculated risk. But in this chapter I'm going to touch a bit on strategizing, collaborating, delegating and branding.

To work smart is to always think a few steps ahead; ask yourself "what if this doesn't go according to plan"...not to scare yourself from moving forward, but to plan for worst case scenario. Working smart means to think bigger, to look at the whole picture and to always ask yourself if there is an easier way, or less expensive way of doing things and then doing them in that fashion. To work smart means to partner with other competent individuals who can help you to get where you're going in a fraction of the time, while also branding yourself (or your company) so you can easily duplicate what you built if you need to rebuild something similar in the future.

BE STRATEGIC

The rich and successful are strategic; they *deliberately* choose their friends, mates, business colleagues, social networks and especially their careers. They are specific about the kind of children their kids hang with, the kind of activities they take part in and the kind of schools they attend. They are very intentional and leave nothing to chance! Do you think it's by chance that they live in certain neighborhoods and enroll their kids in certain schools? The answer is: No. They enroll their kids in certain schools, so they can rub shoulders with certain people so they can continue to marry a certain way and carry on their legacy. So...you too have to learn to purposefully navigate through the system you were born into...if you want to get ahead.

Even though they "say" schools are not segregated anymore, they still are. *They are segregated by income.* Yes technically your children can attend any school you wish...if you can afford it...or if you live in a neighborhood that school is zoned for. Which essentially sentences the poor and middle class to below average schools at best. Because if you don't make a lot of money, you are forced to live in a neighborhood that has higher crime rates, fewer resources, fewer opportunities for advancement and below average schools. At least now, (after much ranting,) there are some schools that will allow you to enroll your child in their school even if your address isn't zoned for it (but most people are unaware of this, and the downside is that they will not provide transportation for those kids). Another thing that most people are unaware of is that most private schools offer financial aid, and in a lot of cases that aid can cover *all* of the tuition if you can prove financial need...which all "poor" people can prove without a doubt. The thing is...most people don't ask or they don't go seeking for that information and these schools don't publicize this info...so most people never find these opportunities. That's why I've taken it upon myself to bring these resources to light...Try it, Google a private school in your area, go on their website and search for a financial aid button or simply call them up and ask if they offer any scholarships or need-based financial aid.

FORM STRATEGIC PARTNERSHIPS

Even Fortune 500 companies are finding that in order to thrive in this economy, they must form alliances. We're in the era of "Co-branding"; Whole companies have merged, look at "FedEx Kinkos" where two separate companies merged to run as one. Between the M&M Company and Mc Donald's the "Mc Flurry", was born. Another co-branded item is: "Virgin MasterCard", some companies now even share the same physical locations like KFC and Taco Bell. What bout Versace brand in H&M stores, or Google Wi-Fi in Starbucks? Apple and Nike did it when they developed an iPod that can communicate with your shoe. Even events are sponsored by other companies now with the agreement to use their name in conjunction with the event like the Blue Cross Blue Shield Florida Classic.

If multibillion dollar companies have come to the realization that they have to work together in order to not become extinct, you too must follow their lead in order the thrive financially.

You can start and run a prosperous business by aligning your company with other companies that are in similar industries but don't have competing products or services. For example, you may make the most scrumptious cakes in town, but as the years go by you see business declining. Perhaps it's because most people can't leave their workplace on their lunch breaks, or most people are too busy to fight through traffic to come all the way to your side of town to pick up their favorite cake. If so, it may be greatly beneficial that you partner with a delivery company and advertise that you now cater; cater for parties and potlucks and your famous cakes can now come to the customer.

CHOOSING THE RIGHT TEAM

With the right team in place you can accomplish your goals in a fraction of the time! Everyone who has achieved success on an enormous scale has had a team. It doesn't matter if it was a team of make-up artists, stylists, accountants, attorneys, assistants, managers, PR agents or just people who believed in them who helped them along the way...but hey had a team!

There is a lot that goes into chasing a dream, building a business or carrying out a mission. There is a lot that you will *not* know, and it will take you a considerable amount of time (perhaps even years) to learn those things. Find comfort in knowing that you don't have to know *everything*; just partner with the people who know what you don't. This will help you to continue to sharpen your natural talents and continue to build on your strongest skills. When forming your team pick other people with different skill sets. For instance, if you're an analytic thinker, a great strategist, organizer and good with numbers then partner with someone who is more creative. You can find out what others are good at, simply by asking them. Or you can ask them what they majored in college or what *would* they have majored in college if they were enrolled.

Choose your teammates wisely. Having the right synergy is mandatory. If you'd like two people to be a part of your team but those two individuals don't get along well, then you have to choose only one. Each disagreement slows down productivity. When choosing members for your team make sure they are people who you can assist in some way, shape or form. As they say: "There is no "I" in team", so this shouldn't be a one-way street. Do something for your team members occasionally to let them know that you truly care about them. You don't have to spend a lot of money to show appreciation. You can cook them dinner, send them a card or recognize them publicly on your social site or website. Those are all small gestures but each one of them means a lot as long as it's coming from a sincere place.

"When building a team you focus on the people who go hard for the team without you asking them to. Not the ones waiting on you"
- P. Diddy

COLLABORATING VS COMPETING

LESSON 45: Losers COMPETE but winners COLLABORATE

I used to think that if I wanted the job done right then I had to do it myself. But now that I am wiser, I realize that no one becomes successful on their own. I now know that if I want the job done right I just have to hire or partner with competent, trustworthy and driven individuals. Although they aren't easy to come by, they are definitely out there. With a little patience and perseverance you'll find the perfect additions to your team. Building your business or carrying out your life's mission is going to require a team effort. Collaborate with people who share your same passions.

LESSON 46: If you can attain your dream all by yourself, then your dream is too small. Dream Bigger!"

THE 3-2-1 FORMULA

Build a strong support group by using the 3-2-1 formula!

<u>LESSON 47</u>: 3+2+1 = Success. 3 people who can teach you, 2 people you can learn with and 1 person you can teach.

<u>Step 1:</u> Seek out (at least) three people who can be your mentors.

These have to be people who have already been where you are trying to go, people who can offer their expertise because of their experience. Their advice will get you where you are going in half the time that it would take you to get to your destination on your own. If you are trying to make a million dollars, seek out a millionaire, if you are trying to start a non-profit, seek out someone who has successfully run a non-profit organization. If you are trying to write your book, then seek out a successful author and ask them to coach you on the book writing and publishing process. If you can't gain direct access to these people, (which may very well be one of your greatest challenges) then read their biographies, Wikipedia or any books they've authored. Read and Google as much as you can about them and watch as many documentaries and YouTube videos of them that you possibly can. If you can't get to them then try to get mentored by anyone in their immediate circle. Because of the "world wide web," you can initiate contact with most people easier than any other time in history. When seeking out your potential mentors, start by visiting their websites; if you find a "contact us" button or are able to locate them on any social media sites then send them a brief but detailed message. Yes your email to them may get lost among the hundreds or thousands...but what if it doesn't? Follow their daily blogs and posts, you never know when they may be hosting an event in your city. Don't be afraid to call their company or show up at their office; tell them how much you admire them and that you'd love the opportunity to be mentored by them.

Make sure you offer them something in return. It could be an acknowledgment in the front of your book once it's finished, it could be goodie bags for their employees stuffed with something that you made, or something that your business sells. You can even offer to run their errands or assist them with their day-to-day affairs. This is where you have to get creative! The whole point of offering your potential mentor something in exchange for them mentoring you (even though they may not need it) is so they realize that 1. You are serious 2. You value their time and you aren't expecting to get anything for free. If you aren't able to offer them anything that would be of value to them, then assure them that you will "pay it forward" to someone in the future who may one day need your help.

From the moment I published my first book, I began to get a lot of requests from people who wanted me to help them write their own books. For the first ten or so people who reached out to me, I was so excited that I started on them right away! I was excited for them because I thought they shared the same passion as I did; a blooming author ready to let the world hear my voice. I'd outline the chapters for them and tell them how to get started and 99% of them *never* followed through. So now I charge people for my services. I don't charge because I *need* their money, I truly love to help people breathe life into their dreams *but* I charge because I hate wasting my time. 99% of the time people won't pay for something that they aren't serious about. So simply by charging, I'm now able to weed out the people who are just "talking" and don't really plan on backing up that talk. Most people didn't want to write their book, truth be told…they just wanted me to write it *for* them!

"Most people don't really want to chase their dream. They want other people to run after it for them!"   – Baje Fletcher

At the end of the day, your potential mentors are just people, they bleed the same blood as you and breathe the same air as you, and the worst that can happen is you get hung up on or get turned away…and a little rejection has never killed anyone. Don't expect this process to be easy. After all, they're successful *because* they are busy…and because they are successful there are people put in place (like receptionist, managers and security guards) to keep people like you away... so approach this mission with resilience, tenacity and armed with a tough skin.

LESSON 48: Mentors hold the blueprint to success.

I recall an encouraging story of Daymond John (founder of FUBU) and how he went to the Trump Towers with the sole intention of meeting his icon, billionaire Donald Trump face to face: only to be swiftly escorted out by security. For most people that would have been a harsh reality check, but that didn't deter Daymond. It actually ignited that burning desire in him even more; he *never* gave up on that goal. It took him some time but one-day opportunity met his drive and he finally had the chance to meet the mogul Trump!

Step 2: Form a partnership with two people who are on your level.

Two people who are just as passionate about success as you are. Two positive people who you can bounce your ideas off of and who will hold you accountable if you start to lose focus. Make it a point to speak with these two accountability partners twice a day. In the morning, share with each other what your goals are for each day and in the evening, share with each other how much of those goals you were able to accomplish.

LESSON 49: When you have someone to report to each day, it gives you more reason to have something to report *about*.

You can even take it a step further by forming a "mastermind group". A mastermind group is a group of people who come together to brainstorm, give unbiased feedback, perfect business and personal skills, educate each other, support each other and hold each other accountable. It's basically a group where members help each other to be successful and get to the next level (whatever that next level may be for each individual). Members challenge each other to set goals and more importantly to accomplish them. Mastermind groups require honesty, commitment, creativity and confidentiality.

When I sent out a post on my social sites for my mastermind group it read something like this:

Forming a mastermind group in Atlanta, Georgia. If you'd like to get together once a week to share ideas with creative, business minded, and driven individuals who are committed to getting ahead, email iLoveBaje@Gmail.com with the subject heading: "Mastermind Group".

You can send out a similar post if you're looking for like-minded people for your mastermind group.

<u>Step 3:</u> Have an apprentice.

You may not think that you've accomplished much in your life so far...but there are people who want to learn what you've already learned and people who want to go where you have already been. Give them that chance. Often we are so caught up on how much more we want to accomplish that we don't realize all that we've accomplished so far. Teach someone what you know and in exchange I'm sure they'll be happy to assist you with some of the smaller things that you need help with: like sending out emails, replying to phone calls and conducting research.

THE POWER OF DELEGATING

Successful people know the power of *delegating*. You are only *one* person: You only have two eyes, two ears, two hands, two feet and one mouth. You can only do so much at any given time. There is power in numbers, learn to tap into that power by *delegating*.

1. Make a list of all the things that you have to do.

2. Then draw a line through each thing that doesn't need to get done. That's right! If you go over that list carefully you'll realize that everything on there won't necessary put you closer to your goal. It's time to pinpoint those things and then eliminate them.

3. Now highlight all the things that need to get done, BUT doesn't necessarily have to be done by you. For instance, you are the one who has to write your book, but someone else can edit it. Or you are the one who has to organize your home office (because you want certain papers in a certain place for easy access) but someone else can organize the rest of the house.

4. Get a *new* sheet of paper and at the top of that page write "Delegate". On this new page, list all of the things that you highlighted from the previous page. It's very important that you have this list neatly prepared ahead of time because you never know when someone will come along who is willing and able to lend a hand. Having this list on hand will save you time and help things to flow smoothly.

5. Make a list of people who you think would be willing to help you with one thing, or even a few things off of that list and actually reach out to

those people. These can be friends who owe you a favor or just have some free time. Even family members who owe you money can probably lend a hand in exchange if they've been having a hard time paying you back. You can reach out to any teens you know who are looking to make a few dollars or any associates who said in the past: "If you need anything let me know". Well...now is the time to let them know. Consider using interns or apprentices. If you have a business, (even if it's a newly established one), there are many students who can gain valuable hand on experience while helping you. There are many free internship sites where you can list the things that your or your company needs help with. If you don't have a company that's still fine. You may not be where you want to be yet, but I'm positive that there are many people who would love to be where you are now. Make it a point to find those people and form win-win partnership. They can offer you hands on help, while you can offer them valuable advice and hands on experience in exchange. You can find interns or just people who would like to learn what you can teach by posting an Ad on the internet, on your social sites at colleges or even on bulletin boards at community centers.

Note: Your list of things to be delegated can be things that are time consuming but still easy enough for someone else to complete. When delegating make sure that you don't delegate tasks to someone new if you have a deadline approaching swiftly because you still need enough time to make corrections if you have to. Finally, never delegate tasks that would put you in a worse predicament if they were to be done incorrectly.

For years I stressed myself out unnecessarily because I thought that if I wanted the job done right I had to do it myself because when I allowed people who reached out to me to help me with projects they would often mess them up. I now realize that I felt that way because in the past I put my trust and my projects in the hands of people who weren't competent for the job. People who were readily available and willing to help, but in hindsight they really didn't posses then necessary skills. The key is to find people who take pride in your work and have just as much passion for the job as you do. If you find yourself having to overly persuade anyone to join your team then those are the wrong people. If someone often misses deadlines, meetings, looses focus easily, or is constantly making excuses on why they weren't able to do what is expected of them, then that isn't someone who you would want working with you or *for you.*

BRANDING

The process involved in creating a unique name and image for a product in the consumer's mind with a consistent theme; The marketing practice of creating a name, symbol, or design that identifies and differentiates a product from other products. Most people don't realize that branding isn't only for businesses; you are a brand. Right now your brand may not be a great one or a big one but you are a brand nonetheless. What is your brand stating? What do people think of when they see you or hear your name? Is what they think in line with what you *want* people to think of you? If the answer to the last question is no, then it's time for you to start elevating your brand. What do you want people to see when they see you coming? What do you want people to think of you? What do you want them to feel when you speak to them? Did you know that a certain phrase you often use could be apart of your brand? Your *name* can be a brand. Your *voice* can be brand. Your *style* of dressing can be a brand, even the way you wear your hair. Find or re-create your brand signature and enhance it. I've even met one man who gives out a gold dollar coin with each of his business cards. That is just his "thing", it's been over ten years since we met, but I still remember him clearly.

If you do have a business, the name of it, your logo and slogan should be on everything. For instance, not only your website, business cards and products, but also your giveaways and shopping bags that you put your customers' purchases in. The key in branding is to be remembered by only a name, image, sound or even color.

NEVER BE FORGOTTEN

"The goal isn't to be noticed, it's to be unforgettable" –Baje Fletcher

I have a mentor by the name of Mr. Jonathan Blount, he happens to be one of the original founder's of Essence Magazine. Every *single* time he introduces himself to someone, his spiel goes like this. "Hello, I'm Jonathan Blount, as in count, as opposed to Blunt as in runt". Not only does everyone find it amusing, they also find it *memorable*. He came up with that line because people often mispronounces his name, he's been using that branding technique successfully for decades now. Jonathan is a well-dressed, well-spoken gentleman with an English accent. He almost never leaves his house without wearing one of his signature hats. Not only can you always spot him in a crowd, but his hats also add flair to his demeanor and tops off his over the top & most importantly *unforgettable* personality.

The Actress Lisa Raye has branded the color white. For the last ten years or so, she has been wearing white exclusively. Elizabeth Taylor is associated with Diamonds. Oprah is known to give away things. Ellen is known for dancing. Halle Berry has branded the short haircut; she found a hairstyle that fits her face and then she owned it. When the singer 'Pink' stepped on the scene she always had pink hair. After solidifying her brand years later she was able to go transition back to her natural hair color, but when she originally stepped on the scene is was memorable. You rarely see Steve Harvey without a suit on. He branded his image so well that he was able to have a successful suit business. *You get the point.*

WHAT DO YOU WANT PEOPLE TO SEE IN YOU?

Take some time to answer that question. If you want to be viewed as *reliable, dependable or trustworthy* it's important that you are on time, keep your word, don't make promises that you keep and possibly give more than what is expected of you.

If you want to be viewed as *a leader* find ways to separate yourself from the pack; For instance, don't engage in gossip, don't repeat things that you can't verify first hand, ask people how you can be of assistance to them and then help those who you can.

If you want to be viewed as *social or outgoing* then take the initiative to introduce yourself to people without them having to ask. Learn to not take rejection personally. It's not about never being rejected, but it's how you handle rejection, and not allowing it to stop you from coming out of your shell.

If you want to be viewed as *confident*, work on your body posture. Walk with your shoulders back and your head held high. Walk intentionally like you know where you're going, instead of slowly and sluggishly. Project your voice while speaking and make eye contact with those you are speaking to.

If you want to be viewed as *intelligent*, then know that the way you dress plays a major part. Get accustomed to wearing suits or even business-casual attire like a blazer or collared shirt instead of a t-shirt, and a pair of pressed slacks instead of jeans or sweatpants. Also, listen more attentively and think of what you want to convey before you speak so that you'll make fewer mistakes.

If you want to be viewed as *independent* then only ask for help when you actually need it. Do as much as you can by yourself before you start seeking outside assistance.

Chapter 6

Have a Screening Process

HAVE A SCREENING PROCESS

<u>LESSON 50</u>: You have to qualify your associates. Everyone can't have access to you...period.

Years ago I made the decision to change my phone number and since then, the only way someone got it was to earn it. Unless I'm giving it to them to discuss business then I need to know their intentions up front. There was a time when I would give my number to just about *anyone* who asked for it. *What's the harm in that? It's just a phone number right?* Well that proved detrimental to my career, to my time and to my piece of mind. People would call me a couple times of day just to check up on me, or see what I was doing now, or to see what I was going to be doing later or see what I did last night. It's great to have people checking in...but not at the price of my future. Almost every call was a distraction, and some of those distractions were cleverly disguised in years of friendship. Every call derailed me from the goals I had set without me even noticing. And then there were the new "friends" who would call me and wake me up out of my sleep late at night when they had too much to drink or were just feeling lonely. Guys I hardly knew were calling me because they wanted to "chill" or because they were "bored" and looking for something to do. My girlfriends were calling me to talk about the latest gossip on MediaTakeOut.com or the popular TV show coming on that night. Party promoters were constantly texting me invites to their weekly events. My phone was ringing constantly...about absolutely nothing! I couldn't get anything of substance accomplished. It was always about what other people wanted. I was being pulled in so many different directions all because I didn't have a screening process.

Then one day it hit me! I had an epiphany! I realized that everyone else was dictating my life...but me. And you know what? Out of all those people constantly calling and texting my phone, I couldn't depend on 90% percent of them for anything! Not for a ride if my car broke down, not to help move furniture when I was relocated, not even to help pay the cell phone bill for the very phone that they were ringing off the hook. *I had to take control of my life.* I changed my phone number and started being real selective about who I gave it to. From that day forward I got real intentional about my circle of friends and associates. I evaluated each person who approached me after that day. *If they used words like "chill", "hang out" & "kick it", they weren't going to make the cut. If they couldn't tell me what some of their goals were they weren't going to make the cut either.* I felt more powerful and felt like I had more control over my destiny when I started making conscious choices about who I was allowing in my life.

When people (particularly guys) approached me and said they wanted to get to know me, instead of just giving them my number upon request, I put them through a mini screening process. 1. I would ask them a little about themselves, 2. I'd ask them what their GOALS in life were and 3. I'd ask them why did they want my phone number. Some of them said, they thought I was "fine" and just wanted to get to know me, shockingly some said that they just wanted to chill and have some fun but weren't looking for anything serious". *(You'd be surprised how blunt people can be if you only ask the right questions).* But the ones who peaked my interest were the ones who said I seemed like a smart woman and they wanted to see if we had anything in common, or see if there was anything we could collaborate on. *So as you can see, there were some clear differences in their intentions.*

As a result of asking a few precise questions, I was able to better gage what each person's intentions with me were. If their response was anything like the first two, I let them know that I wasn't interested. Even if their response was more up my alley (like the third example) I still didn't give them my number. I took their number instead, and when I did call them, I did so *private* the first few times. I wanted to see what direction the conversation would go in, (just in case they were putting on a show the first time we spoke and were trying to disguise pleasure wrapped in business).

When it's evident that you value your time and privacy others will too. You will *not* be the one they choose to call when they're bored, lonely, want to gossip or fill up the next party that they are throwing. Now when my phone rings, I know it's business, or someone who knows me well enough to respect my time. When I made the decision to take control of my life, I had more time to focus on me, my GOALS, and the things that I needed to get done.

LESSON 51: Unproductive friendships have expiration dates.

Because a person started out being a great friend *to you* doesn't always mean that they are going to be a great friend *for you* for the rest of your life. The hardest person to let go is someone who was there for you when you needed them or someone who did something good for you when you first met. So it's easy to use the excuse "He used to be there for me", but what about now? People change, as they are expected to. It's apart of life, but when their change of direction is hindering your growth then it's time to let them go.

LESSON 52: Some people are in your life for a reason, some for a season, and in rare cases...for a lifetime. Decipher the difference.

Everyone in your life does not belong there. Just because you met someone, or were introduced to someone, or because someone *wants* to be in your circle doesn't mean that they automatically belong there. And it sure doesn't mean that they have your best interest at heart so it's up to you to find out if they are going to help you move forward or are they going to hold you back, and then act accordingly.

THE HELP THAT HURTS

LESSON 53: Intentions don't matter, only results do.

Do you have that one friend who tries to help you, but every time he does something goes wrong? What about the friend who always gets pulled over by the cops when you both are out? Or even that one friend, who brings the losing streak to the casino table every single time? Call it a sign or call it superstition, but call it to your attention, and put some distance in between you both until things change back in your favor.

"Trust the vibes you get, energy never lies"

Have you ever had someone in your life who was willing to help with anything you asked for? Or always extended their assistance even when you didn't ask, but they would *always* mess things up? I had a few of those people in my circle and even though it took me years to wean them out of my life I was finally able to. Letting go of these kind people will not be easy, because they care about you and genuinely want you to succeed but you have to. You don't have to let them go abruptly but you *do* have to let them go because it's pointless for them to help you take one step forward when it's going to cost you ten steps back.

I had this one friend, let's call him Robert. He was always willing to help but almost every time he did, something went wrong. If I ignored my instincts and allowed him to help then things often ended up in chaos. If I accepted his help on one of my projects then I was almost sure to have to up clean up after him. If I used one of his referrals then who ever he referred to me ended up messing up my projects as well (perhaps because they thought alike). For example, one time I needed something out of my car and asked him to get it for me, well he locked the keys in the car. Not only did I have to pay for Pop-A-Lock to come and open my door, but I was also late for my speaking engagement; the same speaking engagement he volunteered to help me with that day so things could run "smoothly". Year after year, it was just incident after incident. It was as if he was just prone to mishaps, and *I* would always have to be the one to pay for them because he never had the money. After about fifteen years I got the point and decided that it was just cheaper to help myself. We've been friends for a long time and I wouldn't have been happy distancing myself completely from him. After speaking with a mutual friend Paul, I came to a conclusion. Paul pointed out that I was entrusting Robert with tasks that were clearly too huge for him. He said that Robert was a great friend to me and he didn't think that it would do any of us justice to end the friendship. He said that by assigning him with so much (even though he was volunteering,) I was setting him up for failure. So, to save our friendship I established some boundaries and decided that I could no longer allow him to help me with business ventures or partner up with me on any important projects for that matter.

HELL ON WHEELS

After living in Los Angeles for a few years I got a full time driver, (for privacy purposes I'll call him Damien). He worked for a limousine company for fifteen years but when he parted from the company he was left without a car or means of income. When we met, we figured we could be assets to each other. I lived in LA but I traveled a lot. While I was in town he would drive me wherever I needed to go; that helped me out a bunch because he was way more familiar with the streets. He knew the town like the back of his hand; we almost never got caught in traffic because he knew all the backstreets. Plus I didn't have to waste time or money looking for parking because he would just drop me off and wait for me I was able to get to my meetings and appointments on time, and that took a load off of my shoulders...temporarily. When I was out of town (which I often was), I would allow Damien to keep my Mercedes and I didn't think much of it.

Well...fast-forward a year later, he sold my valuables out of my glove compartment, (which he denied, but I later found out the truth through a mutual friend). Unbeknownst to me, he occasionally drove under the influence of alcohol. He accumulated thousands of dollars of parking tickets on my car and got my car impounded. It wasn't until weeks later when I arrived back home from an out of town trip that he told me what happened! Every time I tried to cut him off, he'd call me repeatedly, send text messages all throughout the day and play on my conscience. "Baje you know I need you, I don't have any family or friends, you are all I have". That worked on me for a while but eventually I found the strength to sever the ties...for good.

"You may not be able to control who comes into your life but you can control how long they stay"

THE VICTIM

It was always something with her. Either she was getting fired, or getting evicted, or going to jail or getting her kids taken away from her, or getting dumped, or getting beat up by her boyfriend. Not saying getting hit was her fault, however, by staying after the first, second, and third time, it was clear that it was now her CHOICE! *(I'll just call her Stephanie).* Almost every single time I spoke to her, she had some drama going on but it was hard to disconnect myself from her because she was one my best friends for almost a decade. Plus she knew where I lived so if she didn't hear from me for a few weeks she would just pop up. Year after year I would comfort her when she was depressed, pawn my jewelry to bail her out of jail, help her move when she got evicted, and extend my home to her and her children when they had nowhere else to go.

I remember one year on Christmas night she popped up at my house. She was hysterical! She was crying, half of her weave was torn out and her clothes were ripped to pieces. After telling her to take some deep breaths and speak slowly, I could start to comprehend what she was saying. She told me that her baby's father beat her up, and dragged her out of his house. Even though I told her numerous times to leave that man alone and she didn't listen I was still furious *at him*. I threw on my coat in a hurry and started putting on my sneakers when one of my family members pulled me to the side and softly said: "Baje, this isn't your battle. You can't leave *your* family for somebody else's. It's Christmas for heaven's sake and we're about to have dinner. Let Stephanie and her family deal with this one". It was a hard decision but I stayed with my family that night. It was unsettling, but I spoke to Stephanie for a while, comforted her, and told her to go home and explain everything to her family and she did.

A few weeks later I received a call from a strange number. "You have a collect call from... *Baje, it's me Stephanie*". She apparently went back on her child's father property even though there was a trespassing warrant previously served to her. She said that things were calm with them for a while so she thought that it was fine for her to stop by. But when she did, he called the police and she was arrested. She couldn't depend on her family to bond her out because they were upset that she went to his house in the first place after they repeatedly told her not to. So guess who had to bail her out? Me. At that point I was thinking, "Why am *I* the first person who people call when they're in jail, or stranded, or in an altercation or when they need money? I realized that it was because I used to have a hard time saying "NO" and actually meaning it.

About a month later Stephanie, my other girlfriend Suzie and myself were planning to go to an event. At the last minute I wasn't able to make it so they went without me. 3 o' clock in the morning I get a phone call from a frantic Suzie, "Oh my God! Baje, Stephanie is crazy! You won't believe what happened tonight. So we were on our way to the event but then Stephanie decided that we should check out this other event instead. So we did and everything was fine for the first hour until Stephanie suggested that we go in the VIP area. Shortly after we were in that section she was arguing with a guy. The next thing I know, security was escorting her out! That's when she told me that the guy she was arguing with was her child's father. And that's when I thought to myself; didn't you tell me that you got locked up over him just the other day?

When we got back to the car and she refused to leave the parking lot when I asked her to take me home. She said she wasn't going to leave until he came out of the event and she got a chance to speak to him face-to-face. Well, after about forty minutes of waiting, he walks out...WITH A WOMAN ON HIS ARM. They hop in his car and take off. Stephanie goes absolutely nuts!! She starts trailing him in her car and calling his cell phone screaming at the top of her lungs! And when he told her to stop following him or he'd call the police. She said that she didn't care about going back to jail.

Let me remind you that this is the same girl that used to constantly come to me playing the victim. The same girl who was still out on bond, on a bond that "I" signed. On a bond attached to *my* checking account so if she didn't show up to court or if she got into any other run-ins with the law thousands of dollars would be deducted from *my* checking account! She clearly didn't care or appreciate me putting my time and money on the line for her. After I had the opportunity to talk to her baby's father I realized that she was the instigator all along. Hearing his side of the story played a decision in me ending our friendship...*unregrettably.*

I grew tired of running around the same circles with her. I finally realized that I couldn't make her (or anyone one for that matter), want better. They have to want better for themselves. I couldn't end our friendship face to face because if I saw her in person I knew I would feel sorry for her and would change my mind. She was one of my best friends, but there came a point when I chose to love myself more. And I couldn't possibly love myself if I allowed people who didn't love themselves to surround me. I had to start letting those people go in order for me to grow into the person that I needed to become.

I wrote her a letter:

Dear Stephanie,

It's not your boss, or your landlord, or your exes, or your baby's father; the problem is YOU! I remember three years ago I told you something that you said hurt you so bad that you didn't talk to me for two months. I told you that five years were going to pass and you were going to be in the same exact place if you didn't make some changes. I didn't mean to hurt you when I said that but it's the God honest truth. Three years have already passed and you have accomplished absolutely nothing. I've tried to be there for you, I tried to motivated you, I tried to show you ways that you could capitalize off of your talent and even though you say that you want a better life you're not doing anything to make that happen. One day you snapped at me and told me that I was pushing you too hard and that you're not like me, and you can't do all the things that I've asked you to do with your life. I was shocked! I NEVER had anyone get angry with me for pushing them too hard. I wish I had someone to push me.

Then you use your children as an excuse saying you could move to a better city or go back to school if you didn't have kids. Women have 3, 4 and 5 kids and still get things accomplished. Why are you so scared to take a chance? If things don't work out you can always go back to the bottom, but at least take the chance! You are still allowing your childhood to hold you back. I know that you were abused as a child but you aren't that helpless child anymore and you have got to stop using your past as a crutch. It was a terrible thing and I am truly sorry that it happened to you but how many more years are you going to be the victim? We all have been victims to someone or something to some degree at some point, but despite of our past circumstances, some of us CHOOSE to be victors. I hope one day you choose to be a victor. Xoxo Baje

LESSON 54: Patterns speak louder than words.

When it's hard for you to make up your mind on what is the best thing for you do to, don't *listen* to people's reasons, just look at their patterns.

THE SQUATTER

Almost a decade ago I was getting my hair done and the stylist Lisa, (I was referred to Lisa by my friend Omera). Lisa and I were in deep conversation about our goals, aspirations and living arrangements, when she told me she was kind of between places and was looking for a room to rent. I told her that in exchange for doing my hair every once in a while, she could stay by me free of charge until she got on her feet because I had space, and traveled a lot so half the time I wasn't even home. When I told Omera about Lisa staying with me, you should have seen the look on her face. She said that she only known Lisa for a year and that I was going to be the fourth roommate that she had! Flags went off in my head but I ignored my intuition as well as that blatant warning. I figured, that everybody goes through hard times at some point and if the shoe were on the other foot I'd hope that someone would extend the same invitation. Perhaps she's just going through a rough patch or rough year, or whatever.

Well, Lisa moved in the next day. I only had two house rules, (no visitors and no smoking in the apartment) which she consistently broke within weeks. After a couple of months it clearly just wasn't going to work for me, but I didn't want to hurt her feelings by telling her that she had to leave. So I let her know when the last day of the lease was approaching, and when the day arrived I packed my things, told her that I was *not* going to renew the lease, (although I had every intention to renew it). I was hoping that she would pack her things and find somewhere else. Well, easier said than done. On the day we were "suppose to" move out, she didn't pack a thing. When I asked her what were her intentions, she said that she spoke to the landlord about taking over the lease and he agreed! As you can imagine I was flabbergasted. I quickly found another place and left her there. As it turned out, she couldn't pay the following month's rent the next month and was evicted. We didn't speak much after that, but we did run into each other once or twice. But six years later, word on the street is that Lisa is still sadly doing the same thing...squatting. This woman is now in her thirties, still bouncing around from one person's home to the other, has never had a consistent job, never had a place of her own, a car or driver's license. I should have listened to Omera, as well as my intuition.

IS BLOOD REALLY THICKER THAT WATER?

It can be extremely difficult for you to let go of people you've known forever, like your family. "Blood is thicker than water". You hear it all the time, but is it really true? I don't subscribe to the "blood is thicker than water" propaganda. I have family members that I've distanced myself from because they didn't have my best interest at heart and then I have a few people I'm friends with but we are inseparable. I know people who were molested by a family member and even beaten and verbally abused on a normal basis. Members of their own family told them that they were nothing, that they'd never amount to anything, and that no one would ever want them. I've seen family turn their backs on family when they were down and out and when they needed help the most. I've seen family put family out in the streets and as a result they were raped. I've seen family lie to each other, steal from each other and manipulate one another. But the worst is when I see families floating in dysfunction and call it "love".

In most cases your family members are the ones who have the ability to hurt you the most because they are the closest people to you. When you can easily brush off harsh words spewed at you from strangers, those same words from your family sink in deep. Even if what they say isn't true, that doesn't stop those poison filled words from seeping in. I've seen family who manipulate each other, family who will never give credit for something that's done right, and would never celebrate another member's success, but can't wait for others to fail or fall just to say "I told you so". Then there are the family members who no matter how much you give to, it's never good enough; *just like a bottomless bucket*. If what I'm saying is hitting home, then listen to me very carefully. That kind of "family" can be lived without. You don't have to live like that. Go on a journey to friends who build you up instead of tear you down & build your own family.

"Blood may be thicker than water, but love is thicker than anything"

Chapter 7

How to Manage Your Time

HOW TO MANAGE YOUR TIME

LESSON 55: Time is more precious than money, for when time is gone you can't get it back.

It's your un-renewable resource, making it your most precious asset. Many people say that they can't *find* enough time to do the things they want but, the truth is, it's not about *finding* time, because if they want those things badly enough, then they will *make* time. *People make time* for things that really matter to them and when it doesn't matter, they *make excuses*.

One pet peeve of mine is when someone calls or texts me saying they just want to see what I'm up to because they're bored. I don't think the word *bored* should exist in anyone's vocabulary. I have a daily "To Do" list that I never have enough time to complete and if I ever did complete all those tasks in one day then I have another never-ending self-improvement list that I tackle if I ever get "spare" time; like a list of self-help & business books to read, tutorials to watch and webinars to listen to.

LESSON 56: Your success will depend directly on your daily routine. The small tasks that you do everyday will make an impact how successful you become in the long run.

I value my time; I despise long waiting periods, especially long hold times on the phone. Whenever I travel, go to the DMV or doctor's office I bring a book with me so I can read while I wait. I realized that by pressing "0" while listening to recordings of most businesses, I am able to bypass the automated system and get a live representative. For the times that method doesn't work, I put the call on speakerphone so I can tackle other tasks. If you always experience an unusually long hold while dealing with big companies, then try choosing a different # option. If you find that when you have to make a complaint, cancel services, or reschedule an appointment you are on hold longer, then press the option to sign up for new services, book a new reservation, or set up a new patient appointment, and get a representative fairly quickly. At least now some of the bigger companies give you the option of having them call you back without losing your place in queue.

GET MORE TIME OUT OF YOUR DAY

Make a list of everything that you usually do on a daily basis and see if there are some things that you can eliminate or try to come up with ways that you can use each hour more effectively. For instance, if you are a stay-at-home mom perhaps you can enroll your kids in a 'before school', 'after school' program or weekend activity like karate, soccer, or tennis so that you have more time to take on other tasks. Often times if you ask the head of extracurricular programs if they have any discounts or offer any kind of financial assistance, they'll accommodate you if you agree not to disclose that help with anyone else. *You never know unless you ask.*

Instead of giving your children an allowance for no specific reason, let them earn their allowance by assisting you with some of light but important tasks like cleaning or organizing. Even if they are younger (like 7 or 8) they can still help with things like picking up stuff around the house. If you have even younger children who don't receive an allowance, introduce them to chores like cleaning up their room and picking up after themselves. The less time you spend picking up after them is the more time you'll have to do more pertinent tasks.

PRE-PLAN

"Time: You can never get it back once it's gone, but you can make more use of it before it comes...by pre-planning"
— *Baje Fletcher*

There are so many things to accomplish in this world; if you have time to be bored you have way too much idle time on your hands or you just don't have your priorities straight. In order to get more time out of your day; there are some free prioritize list templates available at http://www.wikihow.com/Sample/Prioritize-Daily.

It's important for you to have a pre-written "To Do" list to work from. (For the people you have to email or call, write down there contact info right there on your list so you save time not having to look each up when you're ready to contact them)

You should do something *every single day* that contributes to your end goal.

Cross off each task or goal promptly; it will give you a sense of accomplishment, and the fortitude to keep accomplishing more.

Plan each day out by the hour; make sure there isn't an hour unaccounted for.

If you find that there isn't enough hours in a day to accomplish what you need to, then try waking up an hour earlier than you normally do or going to bed an hour later.

Planning out your day from the night before is effective, because you can hit the ground running when you wake up.

Have deadlines & time frames. For example, when you do schedule meetings, schedule an end time as well. For instance, instead of telling someone that you can meet with them at 2pm, let them know that you have an opening from 2pm to 2:30; that way they'll know that their time is limited.

You'll get more hours out of your day if you break your "To Do" list down by categories, like phone calls you have to make, things you have to do on the internet and thing you have to do physically...like running errands. So you know that if you are not near the Internet you can easily start to make the calls you have to make by just reviewing that organized section.

The first thing you should do when you wake up, (besides thank God for waking you up), is visualize what you want your day to be like. Or visually do a walk through of the things that you have to do. Because when the time comes for you to actually do them, you'll be able to do them quicker because you've seen yourself doing them already.

Plan to check email only once or twice a day...but and not first thing in the morning. Nine times out of ten every email that comes in is requesting that you do something, or for you to visit another web page. It's just too easy to get tied up in what others want of you, rather than what you need to do for yourself.

Always write down your meetings and appointments in a planner, on a calendar, or set reminders for them on your phone...even if it's a quick meeting or even if you think you wouldn't dare forget something that important. Also set a reminder alarm a day and an hour before the meeting. Being prepared in advance cuts down on lost time.

"The shortest pencil is better than the longest memory"

LESSON 57: Just because you are busy doesn't mean you're productive.

GET ORGANIZED

"I've never met someone who was successful, who wasn't organized"
-Baje Fletcher

Start small; don't overwhelm yourself because organizing is a life long habit. Being organized not only saves you time but it puts you in a clearer frame of mind as well. When your mind isn't at ease, when you are going through something mentally like depression, anxiety, a midlife crisis or a transitioning period in your life, it reflects in your work, surroundings, environment, hygiene and even the way you dress. If you are going through something (or even if you aren't), things run a lot smoother when you are organized and have some sort of order in your life. If you aren't getting the results that you want out of life, try working on your organization skills.

Stop procrastinating! Narrow down what you *need* to do and then get it done. Notice that I didn't say: What you want to do…but what you *need* to do.

Organize your "To Do" list. Tackling the hardest things first will make it easier to take on everything else. Or list everything in the order of importance or in chronological order of how you'll complete each task.

Not only organize your "To Do" list, but also organize your laptop, home office and car. You'll be amazed at how many minutes you can accumulate in each day by not wasting them looking for misplaced files and items.

Group contacts in your phone and on social sites by category, or city or by friends, family, co-worker or by any grouping system that will make it easier to locate the group when you have to send mass messages or invites.

Backup all your information from your computer and phone to the icloud, a hard drive, Time Machine or any other reliable software. There is no bigger waste of time than having to find other means to retrieve lost contacts and important files.

If you use a notebook for your daily notes or "To Do" list, take a photo of it, so just in case you lose your notebook or forget it you aren't thrown off track. If your "To Do" list is electronic, then back it up.

Get twelve envelops and write one month on each of them. Save all your receipts in the correlating envelope that month. (By keeping your receipts in one place, you'll be able to easily track your expenditures more accurately while going over your budget each month).

Sign up for auto-pay to pay your bills. You have to pay your bills each month anyway, so might as well save some time doing it. Some companies even offer you discounts for paying automatically and it will also save you money by not having to buy a money order or pay additional fees by paying over the phone.

Organizing your environment, keeping things neat, clean, and clear of clutter in your home, car and workspace will also clear your mind.

Use a portable folder filer for all your paper work, instead of using a stationary cabinet file, so you can easily stow it away in a closet or under a desk when you're not using it.

Create more space by capturing photos of your children's 3-D projects instead of storing them.

You can use clear shoe organizers for jewelry, hair accessories and toiletries.

Make good use of Ziploc bags, they're great to organize and store more things than just food.

Staying organized has a lot to do with how you feel, so decorate your work and living spaces with inspirational and motivational images, quotes or even colors that make you feel happy in order to keep you on track.

Use Apps like "Unstuck" to help you get organized.

MANAGING YOUR HABITS

You may know me.
I'm your constant companion.
I'm your greatest helper; I'm your heaviest burden.
I will push you onward or drag you down to failure.
I am at your command.
Half the tasks you do might as well be turned over to me.
I'm able to do them quickly, and I'm able to do them the same every time, if that's what you want.
I'm easily managed; all you've got to do is be firm with me.
Show me exactly how you want it done; after a few lessons I'll do it automatically.
I am the servant of all great men and women; of course, I'm the servant of all the failures as well.
I've made all the winners who have ever lived.
And, I've made all the losers too.
But I work with all the precision of a marvelous computer with the intelligence of a human being.
You may run me for profit, or you may run me to ruin; it makes no difference to me.
Take me. Be easy with me, and I will destroy you.
Be firm with me, and I'll put the world at your feet.
Who am I?
I'm Habit!

          - Dennis Waitley

<u>LESSON 58:</u> Nothing will create more time for you than cultivating the habit of discipline.

"Motivation is what gets you started, habit is what keeps you going.
–Jim Rohn

In fact, when it comes to productivity, knowing which tasks to eliminate completely may be more effective than actually doing the things that you think "need" to be done. Your habits are the biggest consumers of your time. Whether or not you realize it, your habits soak up your time like a sponge; Analyze the little things you do on a daily basis that aren't necessary and then completely remove them from your daily routine.

Each time you participate in doing something trivial or something that you don't *need* to do (no matter how small it may be) it takes time away from doing the more important things that you need to be doing. You may not see danger in one small frivolous activity, but each time you partake in just one more you're forming an unproductive habit. Breaking habits is a process; it usually doesn't can't be broken overnight, but start by consciously doing more of what *you do want* and less of what you do NOT want and before you know it that habit will be broken.

At the end of each day take some time to reflect on all of the activities that you took part in, then add up the time you spent on each activity that didn't contribute to you getting ahead, e.g. gossiping with friends, watching TV solely for entertainment and not educational purposes, reading entertainment/celebrity blogs (like TMZ, Bossip and Media Take Out), looking up YouTube videos that had nothing to do with your goals, surfing the internet mindlessly, sleeping and Facebook stalking your Ex.   Now tally up those minutes; then multiply that number by thirty, that's how many minutes you wasted this month!

Make a commitment to eliminate trivial activities from your daily routine. When you have downtime try to work on your 'To Do' list, or read self-help books, or financial magazines such as Money, Entrepreneur, The Economist or Black Enterprise. If you find yourself with extra time on your hands, instead of surfing social sites, look up tutorials on YouTube that can actually teach you a skill or something of importance. Even look up motivational speakers like Les Brown, Tony Robbins or Eric Thomas who will help to inspire you to reach your full potential. Instead of listening to the radio on your way to work make the switch and put in an audio book. Instead of reading tabloids and blogs about celebrities, try reading the biography or Wikipedia of someone empowering who you look up to and see if you can follow in their footsteps.

NOT "TO DO LIST"

Having a NOT "To Do" list, is just as important as having a "To Do" list. In most cases it's not that there isn't enough hours in a day, it's that we spend our time doing things that aren't getting us ahead. Take a few minutes to analyze the last week of your life, identify your time-wasting patterns and try to find way to correct them.

Do not check your email first thing in the morning.

Do not check your social sites first thing in the morning.

Do not keep the ringer on your phone when you have a deadline.

Do not take personal calls within business hours.

Do not connect to WIFI if you are working on the computer and the project doesn't require you to connect to the Internet (it will be too easy to get distracted aimlessly surfing the Internet).

Do not read the newspaper or watch the news, especially first thing in the morning (90% of what's reported is negative and depressing and it subconsciously drains your mood). If something huge is in the news that will directly impact your life, trust me, you'll hear the news from your family and friends.

Do not visit Celebrity news and gossip sites. Really, how does that contribute to you getting ahead? (Unless you blog for a living...it doesn't). Celebrities already found their success; it's time for you to get yours.

Do not make sports the center of your life. I get that you need a release from time to time, but when it's sports season and you're constantly glued to the TV or you attend every single game, that's time away from your goals. These basketball and football players already have their million dollar contracts; it's time for you to get *your* millions and if you sported a shirt with the name of your *own* business, as often and proudly as you do their jersey's, you'd be a lot closer to your millions.

SAY NO WITHOUT FEELING GUILTY

LESSON 59: Sometimes you that have to say NO, and be absolutely fine with that.

You'd be surprised how much time you can save by simply saying "No". Are you one of those people who'd spend up to ten minutes on the telephone listening to a telemarketer because you don't have the courage to cut them off in the middle of their spiel and say that you're not interested? Those three minutes here and six minutes there really do add up.

Are you the one that your friends appoint to tag along every time there is a party just so you can be the designated driver? It's ok to say no and stay home and do something productive. You don't have to feel guilty; they'll find someone else.

Are you one of those people who puts everyone else's needs before your own and as a result the things you need to do hardly get done on time? You don't have to be stressed. Just learn to politely say no. If those people really care about you they'll understand that you have a life and responsibilities as well.

Make a conscious decision to not waste time in activities and conversations that do not get you ahead in life. We all have that one friend who call us or pops up a few times a day just to see what we are doing or just to *talk...about anything* (most of the time...nothing...of substance anyway). Don't be afraid to interject in the one sided conversation; a simple "I'm sorry I was in the middle of something", or "I'm sorry I'm working on something and have a deadline to meet" usually gets the point across.

At first it may be hard to break your bad time management habits but the more you work on them, then the easier it will get.

MANAGING TIME IN A DIGITAL AGE

LESSON 60: Social media can make you or break you!

Devoting a lot of time on social sites (like Twitter and Facebook) can either build you up or break you down. A few of my friends deleted their Facebook pages; They said that it was a distraction and a complete waste of time and they didn't see many owners of fortune 500 companies tweeting and tagging on these social sites. I beg to disagree, I don't think it's having an account or being on a social site that creates the problem, but a lack of self-discipline. Rather it's what you do *while* you are on these sites that makes all the difference.

For instance, I use my social sites to promote my businesses, products and to give inspirational quotes of the day. I hardly ever visit other people's pages or read through their daily posts unless I have a specific reason to, because most people just use the tool to spread rumors, jokes, gossip and their relationship issues. It's easy to get caught up in the hype and the 'joneses'. But if you're disciplined enough not to, then social networking is one of the most powerful and affordable tools that you'll ever have access to.

It's a known fact that a huge reason why President Obama won his first and second presidency race was because he marketed effectively on social sites like Facebook, YouTube and Twitter. And though you may not see the *owners* of Fortune 500 companies on social sites you better believe that they have thousands and thousands of people on those site promoting their products.

LESSON 61: You can't get more time, but you can use the time that you do have more effectively.

USING SOCIAL MEDIA TO GET AHEAD

Use your social sites to cross promote on other social sites.

1. You can pre-schedule your tweets to go out automatically.
2. You can schedule your Tweets from Twitter to automatically post to your Facebook.

3. You can simultaneously post to Facebook, Twitter, Tumblr, Flickr & Foursquare from Instagram.

4. You can send an automatic alert to your Twitter timeline every time you upload a video to YouTube.

5. You can link your social sites to your mobile phone.

6. You can set auto responders.

7. Best of all, you can view & manage multiple social sites on one dashboard using some social site managers.

SOCIAL SITE MANAGERS

Hootsuite uses one dashboard to schedule Tweets and Facebook posts and if you have a company now you can share your workload amongst teams, departments, or regions. Assign tasks, receive real-time notifications, and have internal conversations right from the dashboard.

With SocialOomp you can Twitter, Facebook (profiles, pages, and groups), LinkedIn (profiles, groups, and company pages), RSS feeds, blogs, Plurk, and App.net! Easily schedule updates.

Buffer helps you to plan a schedule that helps optimize Twitter updates by scheduling them and spreading them out throughout the day.

TwitterFeed does more than just cater to your Twitter account. Webmasters and bloggers can effortlessly update their social media accounts with new RSS feed posts by integrating TwitterFeed into their social accounts. RSS feeds can be connected to Twitter, Facebook, LinkedIn, StatusNet and HelloTxt for automatic updating.

With Tweetdeck you can monitor multiple timelines in one easy interface, manage multiple Twitter accounts, schedule Tweets to be posted in the future, turn on alerts to keep up with emerging information, filter searches based on criteria like engagement, users and content type, build and export custom timelines to put on your website, use intuitive keyboard shortcuts for efficient navigation and never hit refresh again: TweetDeck timelines stream in real-time.

Like TweetDeck, Seesmic has app integration for practically every major platform out there, both mobile and web-based. Streams from your networks can be processed and viewed in an interface that resembles typical email platform.

IFTTT is a powerful Internet automation site that can save you a lot of time managing social media and other tasks through recipes. You can essentially connect any major network or channel together to automate sharing on sites like Facebook, Twitter, LinkedIn and more based on any action you desire. Like sending out a tweet automatically every time you publish a new blog post.

AUTOMATE YOUR LIFE

Set up an automated backup program like "CCleaner" on your computer once and it will automatically back up your data so you don't have to worry about it getting lost.
If you've got antivirus software you can set up automatic tune-ups and maintenance.

Using "Automator" for Mac, or "Actions" for Window will let you automatically rename a group of files, crop a large number of images, and even extract text from a bunch of PDF files saving your precious time.

If you have an iPhone make use of "Siri". She'll get directions, call anyone in your phonebook, send a text, check your voicemail or email, tell you the temperature outside, play a song you request or Google anything simply by telling her to…no typing required.

Signing up for automatic bill pay with your bank and service providers will eliminate you spending time each month to pay bills.

Sign up for reward programs with grocery stores. They're usually free and will eradicate coupon clipping. Just by scanning your rewards card at the checkout counter you'll automatically get all the discounts and rewards you qualify for.

Amazon now has its "Subscribe and Save" program, where you can pay to have your regularly used items (like toiletries) shipped to you automatically, at a discounted rate. It will save you the frustration of scrambling to get things last minute.

There are tons of ways you can even automate your home using your smart phone and other gadgets, like having keyless entry, adjusting your thermostat, cleaning your floor, feeding your pets, dimming your lights and monitoring your home.

On www.producthunt.com/e/automate-your-life there is a wealth of tools and information on automation.

Performing a simple Google search of "How to automate my life or home" will give you many more options.

PRIORITIZE

Be a self-starter. Don't wait for anyone else tells you what needs to be done. Just take the initiative to do it.

Unwind before you tackle your daily "To Do" list. Often times just looking at your list of things to do can be a bit overwhelming, so do something that puts your mind and body at ease: like saying a praying, taking a hot shower, taking a bubble bath, lighting some scented candles, drinking some hot tea or listening to some music.

Rank your projects. Get a notebook and write down all the things you need to get done that day or week. Put a star beside the top five important things that you have to accomplish first and tackle them immediately. Then number the other remaining projects in the order in which you want to tackle them…then start tackling.

First tackle the things that will generate the most money or free up more of your time.

Resist the urge to check email, voicemail and your social sites before you start tackling your list each day. If not, you'll start your day doing what others want you to do, opposed to what you need to do for yourself.

Don't multitask. Do one task a time, because just like how your computer slows down when you have a lot of windows open, that's just how your brain gets frozen and doesn't work to the best of its ability when you are trying to concentrate on more than one thing at a time.

Group your list by the type of things you have to do. Make all your phone calls at one time, do all your house chores at the same time, run all your errands at the same time, reply to all your emails at the same time, do all your shopping at the same time and pay all your bills at the same time.

Know when to drop the excess. Look over your list from top to bottom, now start crossing off the meaningless stuff. If you look at it long enough you'll realize that a good third of those things aren't really necessary.

BE PROFICIENT

An unmade bed can make a whole room look untidy; so spread your bed as soon as you get out of it, it's one of the small things you can do to set the tone for the rest of the day.

Make a habit of putting things right back after you use them.

Make a daily to-do list and bring it with you everywhere throughout the day. It can be Post-it notes, an organizer, an iPad, the memo section of your phone, a word document on your laptop or just a regular notebook.

Keep a pad and pencil on your nightstand in case you get any great ideas in the middle of the night. At first they may seem like random thoughts, but by collecting your thoughts on paper, over a few months you might start finding some synergy.

Have "schedule agendas" and have each hour accounted for
Make a list of your short term and long-term lists/goals & keep them on a wall in the room that you spend the most time.

Trick your brain by acting like you only have less time to get things done, or try setting a time limit, or even a *timer* for each task.

Set two reminders for time sensitive things, or ask a reliable friend to remind you about important events.

Delegate everything that you don't have to do yourself to someone dependable. If you don't have anyone dependable in your immediate circle, consider getting an assistant on www.FancyHands.com for as low as $29 a month.

Give children their own alarm clocks and encourage them to wake up on their own. Post a checklist in your kid's room of things they need to complete each day. (It'll cut down on how many times you'd have to verbally reintegrate it).

Put kids snacks and eating utensils in a lower kitchen cabinet, (that way they can feed themselves).

Have a two-compartment laundry baskets so that you can sort light clothes from dark clothes while you're undressing.

Have a clock in all of your bathrooms so you are mindful of the time while you are getting ready.

Make a kit for the small (but vital) things that you usually spend ten minutes looking for while trying to rush out of the house each morning. Like gum, mints, hair ties, hairpins, safety pins, tweezers, nail clippers and your favorite pair of earrings.

Choose keys with different patterns or designs on them instead of a normal gold or silver key. It will create less confusion and save you time.

Use removable key rings, so you can easily separate your home key from your car keys, in case you have to leave keys with someone else like the valet, babysitter or pet sitter.

Save time in the mornings by picking out the day's outfit the night before.

Ask your creditors to change the due dates of your bills so you can pay them all on the same day.

Get three boxes and sort things as you clean up your home or workspace. One box is for things you can sell (whether at a garage sale or online, like on eBay and Craigslist.) the next box is for things you want to give away and the last box is for trash.

BE PREPARED

Always have backups of important things, like a set of spare house keys, and car keys.

Keep a bag or small suitcase in your car's trunk so you can keep a business outfit, casual outfit and gym outfit in it. Just in case one day you are stuck in traffic and can't make it home to change on time, or if something else comes up last minute you are prepared. Also keep an extra toothbrush and deodorant in there also.

Create a checklist that other family members or your babysitter can use as a guideline in case they need to step in and takeover for you. E.g. what goes in your child's overnight bag and what to pack in your child's lunchbox.

Have all your passcodes and account #'s written down in one place where you can easily access them.

Write down your debit / credit card number in case you leave it at home and you need to make a purchase. In some cases you can just tell the merchant your card #, expiration date and three-digit security code and they'll punch it in to their system to complete your purchase.

Put important documents like social security cards, birth certificates, house title, car title, passports, immunizations cards, life insurance & other information, in a briefcase (preferably water & fireproof, so that if there is an emergency, you can just grab it and run. (Documents like those aren't easily replaced).

Have your whole family know where the easiest exit and safest hiding spot is in your home is, in case of an emergency or break-in.

Show your family members where you keep your weapons, fire extinguisher, flashlights, candles & matches in case you have a break-in or emergency.

Have a run through emergency drill with your whole family.

Leave a list of emergency contact numbers taped to your fridge.

Have one person in the family know what company your life insurance policy is with, which attorney has a copy of your will and where to locate all the passwords to your bank accounts in case something should ever happen to you.

"You deserve to save time because time is money, & you deserve to save money because you earned it."
- Baje Fletcher

Chapter 8

Learn What Schools Don't Teach
...About Money

LEARN WHAT SCHOOLS DON'T TEACH
... ABOUT MONEY

LESSON 62: Money is always there; it's just the pockets that change.

In fact, there is a saying that goes, "If you divided all the money in the world evenly among everyone on earth, within a few years the same amount would all end up back in the same pockets". This is true because *money is a mindset.* Money is a reflection of your habits, your self worth, and your level of discipline.

"If you want to know your beliefs about money, take a look at your bank account"

On my journey to become financially literate and financially free, I've read any finance book that I could get my hands on. I watched hundreds of hours of videos on finances and picked the brains of many financial experts. No matter the source of the information, there were certain rules that were consistent all across the board. Though none of these individual rules are hard to achieve, our *habits* make mastering money difficult. The key is to master one rule before you take on another. If you take on the whole list at once it may seem overwhelming, but if you tackle it step by step then you'll get closer and closer to mastering the game of money.

Financial Literacy: Is the ability to understand how money works in the world: how someone earns it or makes it, manages it, donates it or turns it into more by investing it.

It's the set of skills and knowledge that allows an individual to make informed and effective decisions with all of their financial resources.

Unfortunately in school we are taught everything we need to know about everything else EXCEPT financial literacy. The date Pearl Harbor was bombed, the distance from the earth to the moon, how to calculate the radius of a circle, but when it comes to what runs the world we live in today (managing cash & credit), it's *conveniently* left out. Perhaps they forgot, or maybe a textbook on "real life finances" just hasn't been written yet...or maybe if the whole world is educated on how to make money, how to keep it and how to make it grow...then the 1% of the world who owns it won't have anyone to work for them...because everyone will be working for themselves and building their own wealth instead! Either way I'm taking it upon myself to educate you on what I've learned about money so far.

INCREASE YOUR FINANCIAL IQ

If you want to get ahead financially, you should start by keeping and organizing records of your expenses and income (like bills, receipts, invoices, taxes filings and pay stubs). You may not know what to do with them now, but you will need them in the future once you start creating a budget or talking to an accountant or tax professional. No matter how many goals you have in life, one of your main goals should be to increase your financial IQ. To increase your financial IQ you need to increase your knowledge on certain things like how to create a budget (or spending plan), the difference between good and bad debt, how to avoid debt, how to effectively manage credit, how to leverage your money & also use O.P.M (other people's money), learn to find the best mortgage for you, creating the best retirement plan, qualifying for loans and more. You can get educated in these areas by reading an arsenal of business and finance books, subscribing to business and finance magazines, speaking to experts in the financial sector like investors, tax preparers, realtors, financial advisors, and even attorneys.

The goal of speaking to financial advisors isn't for you to fork over all your money to them, but to learn from them. If after you financially educate yourself, you still plan on using a financial advisor to manage or invest your money that's fine; at least then you'll actually *know* what is happening to your money and not just speculating. If you fully rely on someone else to essentially manage your money and solve your financial problems, you can't increase your financial intelligence.

Sometimes financial professionals try to push products on you that are not particularly right for you. So just because you are talking with them doesn't mean that you should feel obligated to buy anything or use their particular services. Sometimes all you need is just enough information to start researching things yourself. Some financial professionals will purposely use terminology that you don't understand to make you feel that they know much more than you, however, you should always ask them for the definition of any word that you don't understand or at least write it down and research it later.

You can go to your local bank and credit union and just ask questions about the different products that they offer and the difference between each product.

There are many helpful websites with a wealth of financial information, MyMoney.gov is one of them; it's a governmental site that teaches the basics about financial education.

Though most schools don't teach you what you need to know to get ahead financially, some colleges may have stand alone non-credited financial classes that you can sign up for to keep abreast of financial matters.

Watch TV…just not mindless TV that doesn't teach you anything. Watch programs like Mad Money, Bank of Mom and Dad, The Barefoot Investor, The Week with Charlie Rose, Money Matters, Squawk Box, Your Money, The Suze Orman Show, The Dave Ramsey Show, Shark Tank, The Profit, and The Bottom Line. If they're no longer on air you can probably watch old episodes online. Watch channels like CNBC, CNN Money, Business Week, Bloomberg TV, Forbes TV, BBC Business and Fox Business Now. (Keep in mind that some of these are online TV channels).

Attend financial seminars and sign up for financial webinars online and tele-seminars over the phone. Listen to online lectures from Suze Orman, Dave Ramsey and Tony Robbins. (Start by looking them up on YouTube).

Some more websites that you will find helpful on your financial quest are FreeMoneyFinance.com, MoneyNing.com, WiseBread.com and MoneyCrashers.com

Download and get familiar with finance apps like Mint.com, Save Benjis, and Shopping List.

With e-books and the Internet you probably forgot that libraries exist, but they do, and books aren't the only resource they have available. For example, the New York Public Library has Money Matters workshops on retirement planning, investing in stocks, interpreting financial statements, budgeting, how to deal with identify theft and more, called "Money Matters Workshops".

Some cities like New York; Nashville, TN; Philadelphia, PA; Denver, CO; Lansing, MI; and San Antonio, TX have Financial Empowerment Centers funded by Cities for Financial Empowerment Fund. They'll provide you with free one-on-one counseling and guidance on issues such as debt management, how to deal with debt collectors, improving credit, building savings and more.

The Federal Deposit Insurance Corporation offers free online computer based instruction (CBI). The CBI features a game-based learning design.

MoneySkill.org offers a free personal finance course for young adults developed by the AFSA Education Foundation. It covers things such as income, expenses, assets, liability and risk management. You'll experience an interactive curriculum as both written text and audio narration.

Make it a mission to seek out at least one successful mentor who you can shadow or be able to call when finance questions arise.

1. Create a budget.

"A budget is telling your money what to do instead of wondering where it went",

This is where wealth begins. A budget is a basic understanding of how much money you're spending versus how much money you're making. You need to physically *see* where your money is going each month, so you can physically record the amount of your bills, or how much you're spending monthly on a sheet of paper, in a notebook, in the memo section of your phone or in an Excel file. It is not only important to see where your money is going, but it is also important for you to allocate a specific amount for each expenditure that you should not go over. Once you see where your money is going then you can assess what is unnecessary and where you can scale back spending. Save all of your receipts. You can label twelve envelopes with each month of the year and file receipts accordingly. (I usually keep my receipt envelope above my car visor for easy access). At the end of the month go through them and see if there was anything that you bought that you didn't necessarily need. Often times it's the small things that add up. I started going through my receipts a few years ago and saw that I spent way too much money on chocolate, energy drinks and weave. After I pinpointed my unnecessary expenditures, then I was able to cut back. I stopped buying chocolate so often, I started buying my energy shots at the dollar store for one dollar instead of five dollars at the convenience store and I started investing in better quality weave that lasted way longer.

Budgeting is all about looking at the bigger picture. In addition to your expenses, it is important that you write down all of your monthly income (whether it is a paycheck, residual check, unemployment check, social security check or child support check). Beside each check amount write down the date you'll receive it. In some cases you may make enough to cover all your expenses, but sometimes the check comes in *after* the bills are due. If that's the case, speak to your creditors to see if they can change your billing date to avoid any late fees or additional interest. You can also download free Aps like (YNAB) "You Need a Budget", "MVelopes" and "Prosper Daily" to help get you on track.

If you have a business, the first thing that you need (besides a written business plan), is to get your bookkeeping in order. There is easy to use accounting software for small businesses like QuickBooks or MYOB. After you are up-to-date and have your information entered into your bookkeeping system, you can generate reports such as a profit/loss report or cash flow projections, which you'll need later on when you're seeking loans or investors.

LESSON 63: It's not how much money you make, it's about how much you keep.

2. Avoid Debt.

Spend within your means! This doesn't mean to live like a tightwad forever, this doesn't mean that you should live like a monk or shouldn't have nice things; but this *does* mean you should wait until you have enough money saved up to buy the things that you want with cash and not on credit. Until then…live within your means, don't stretch yourself too much financially. By spending within your means you'll be able to increase your savings…and by increasing your savings you can start paying down debt and start investing. Smart people live within their means while they are thinking of ways to expand their means; the wealthy understand this principle. The rich stay rich because even when their income goes up their expenses remain the same. Just because you can afford something doesn't mean you have to have it. If you're spending more money because you have more money coming in then pretty soon you'll have nothing left.

Someone I knew, lets call him Maurice, won a settlement of $150,000 a few years ago. His lawyer told him not to keep all his money in one bank account and to take extra measures in order for him to not be able to access his money easily to avoid impulse purchases. He didn't listen. He thought that he could "handle" it. After all...he was an adult right? Wrong! It's not about age or even intelligence but it's about wisdom and discipline. And in this case...*financial* wisdom. Though we all say that if we had that amount of money we'd know exactly how we would use it. Is that really the case? With no financial experience or sound financial advice it's easy to lose all you have because your mindset would still be the same. I heard that more than 80% of people who win the lottery end up going broke in a just few years because they never learned the rules to govern money.

Start paying attention! You may not spend a hundred dollar bill on one single item like a leather jacket...but...what if you had three $20 bills and four $10 bills? Having all those bills may make you feel like you actually have more than you do; so you spend a twenty here and then spend a few ten's there and before you know it all the money is gone. To prevent this, start asking for larger bills when you do get cash back.

Pay attention! Perhaps your problem isn't that you spend money on big purchases, but you squander a lot of money on smaller unnecessary purchases. You may think you're cutting costs because you're buying things from a thrift store, flee market, dollar store, consignment store, or on "Sale"… but if it's things that you don't "need", then it's still a waste of money. Those three dollars here and five dollars there spent frequently on smaller items add up and those little additions can make all the difference in stopping you from reaching your financial goals.

Pay attention! Perhaps you find that when you use your debit card to pay for purchases you end up buying more things more frequently because your brain doesn't link the "plastic" to "money" like it would do with "cash". If that is the case, then use cash for your purchases instead of using a card.

Sometimes you can't get ahead because *you* are working against '*you*'. You'd be surprised at how many people think they can't get ahead because of their finances or location or current circumstances, when in fact there is absolutely nothing in their way but themselves. Are you one of those people? Most of the time it's not how little money or resources you have that is holding you back, but it's how you use the little resources that you do have. If you are down to your last $50, do you spend it on a pair or shoes to make yourself feel better? Do you spend it instead of putting it in a savings account because you think that it's too little to make an impact? Or do you make the sacrifice and *invest* it in you or your business perhaps by purchasing some business cards, taking a potential client to lunch, or buying two books that can teach you how to brand yourself or market your business? *Even when you are on your last dollar...you should think long term.*

"There is good debt, and then there is bad debt".

The difference between good debt and bad debt is that good debt helps you to generate income and increases your net worth and bad debt is...just debt. Some good debt incudes: 1. Student loans (if you can find a great paying job to repay them and make more money on top of that). 2. A mortgage (You're always going to need a place to live, so you might as well own it and besides that you can sell it for a profit or you can rent it out.) And 3. A business loan so that you can generate more money). Examples of bad debt include car loans, credit cards and store credit.

"Keep your dollars for as long as you can, or at least until you have a plan"
— Baje Fletcher

3. Pay yourself first.

You have to develop a habit of paying yourself first, otherwise you'll find that you'll pay your landlord, bill collectors and the government and you'll have nothing left for you to save. You WILL find a way to pay your landlord, bill collectors and government because we humans have the gift of being super creative when the roof over our heads or our freedom is in jeopardy. There are grace periods, extensions, payment plans and payment arrangements; trust me, you'll find a way.

4. Save at least 10% of your income.

You have to pay yourself a certain percentage of all money that you earn; the universally accepted amount is 10%. Once you've mastered the 10% you can increase it to 15% and then 20%. Raising it to 20% is especially important if you are an entrepreneur because you don't have the safety net that most nine-to-fivers have...like an employer to make contributions to your 401k's. You can save cash in an envelope at home, or you can open a savings account at a bank, or credit union or you can come up with your own creative saving strategy. A few years ago I did a "money order system"; every time I earned money I got a money order for 10% of that amount and dropped it in the mail to my sister. She would collect all the envelopes and keep them for me, and every few months I'd get them from her and deposit them in an investment account. This system helped me to not spend the money...because I physically couldn't. If you did decide to do something like this then, 1. Make sure it's someone you trust 2. Fill out the money order with your name so no one else can cash it and 3. Keep the money order stubs and receipts in case any of them get lost in the mail.

5. Make your savings automatic.

See if your bank can automatically deposit a portion of your paycheck to your savings or investment account. You have to come up with ways to trick your mind into thinking that you have less money. If it's automatically deducted out of your paycheck and you don't get to see it then that decreases the chances of you spending it. Here is another little trick that I use personally: I have online banking and when I log into my account I can see the balance in my savings as well as my checking, but I asked my bank to delete my savings account from my online banking. That way I'm not constantly reminded of how much money I have in savings and won't be too tempted to spend it. Some banks have a variety of accounts that suit different saving styles. Call around and ask them about the different kind of automatic savings plans that they offer. Some banks have "holiday accounts"; with those accounts they take a certain amount of money out of your paycheck every pay period so that when Christmas rolls around you have a large lump sum in that holiday account. One bank I was with had a "5K savings plan," where they would take a certain amount out of my regular savings account each month and automatically transfer it to that 5k savings until it reached $5000. They even added an additional feature that discouraged me from making any withdrawals before I reached my 5k goal... which was a fee of $10 per withdrawal; so you know I wasn't making any withdrawals unless it was an absolute emergency.

6. Don't put a cap on your income.

Never work for an hourly rate only. There are only so many hours in a day and if you are only working for an hourly rate you'll never be able to earn over a certain amount. If you have a hand in directly generating income for a person or business try to negotiate a percentage of the money that you have coming in. If you have a goal of starting you own business but you decided to get a regular job temporarily so you can generate income to get your business going, then consider a job in sales, because you won't only be getting an hourly rate but you'll get a commission on everything you sell as well. Just make sure it's a product you'd be proud to use yourself.

"Success isn't only measured in money, it's also measured in happiness" –Baje Fletcher

7. Do what you love!

I know you've heard the phrase a thousand times "Do what you love and the money will come". It's cliché but it's so true. Never, ever, ever get in *any* particular line of business only because it pays a lot of money; you'll be miserable. And after the novelty wears off you'll dread each hour you're working passionlessly; you *will* absolutely regret it. In order to be successful in any field you have to spend thousands and thousands of hours studying, researching, working at your craft and learning from trial and error. In order to excel at anything you have to give it more than the mediocre 40 hours a week. So when you absolutely *love* what you do, you'll be excited to jump out of bed each morning to start working on it, you'll stay up many late nights to continue working on it, you'll skip lunch, you'll put your social life on hold and you'll put every penny you have into it...and you know what...it's going to take all that and more to become successful. So choose to do what you love and it won't feel like work, and because you love what you're doing you'll put in overtime ...all the time, and that's what it's going to take.

"Time is more valuable than money. You can get more money, but you cannot get more time". —Jim Rohn

8. Don't work for money; let it work for you.

Once you've created a written budget to see how much money is going in and how much is going out; and once you've mastered your spending habits and have accumulated savings, it's time to put that money to work! It doesn't matter how much money you make if you're not free to enjoy it. Getting two days off a week and two weeks off a year out of your own life sounds a lot like bondage or blackmail. If it's something you're passionate about or if it's something that's getting you closer to your goals that's different.

For example, if you want to open your business one day so you work at a similar business to gain experience or started building your network and database then that's a great move. Or if you want to see the world so you get a job for a while as a flight attendant so you can travel for free that's also great, but if you're at a job that you hate and you're just doing it for a paycheck you're essentially selling your soul. Furthermore, with most jobs that pay great, they come with the responsibilities, the time constraints and the stress to match! What's the point of making a great amount of money if you aren't happy and you can't enjoy it?

"Working is the worst way to make money"

Working is the worst way to make money and successful people know this, that's why they make their *money work for them!* There are three things that successful people do to ensure that they not only make money but also have the time to *enjoy* it.

1. They BUILD BUSINESSES & hire competent employees to run them.

2. They INVEST their money & live off of the Interest, Capital Gains or Dividends.

3. They CREATE STREAMS OF PASSIVE & RESIDUAL INCOME.

"Money makes you rich, but Money AND time makes you wealthy"   *–Baje Fletcher*

1. BUILDING BUSINESSES

Though being self-employed puts you in a better position than being an employee, and though you can even make your own schedule, in most cases, you're still trading your time for money. So, if you got sick or wanted to take a vacation or had to deal with personal or family issues, your income would stop for as long as you're away. The benefit of building a business is that it can still make money while you aren't present. There are a few ways successful people run businesses.

- Sometimes they buyout or takeover existing businesses.

- Sometimes they purchase franchises. (A franchise is usually a business chain that grants the license to a third party the right to conduct a business under their trademark and trade name). Purchasing a franchise is one of the easiest ways providing you have the funds, because usually the brand is already well known and you have strict guidelines to follow that will increase your chances of being profitable.

- And a lot of times they start a business from the ground up.

If you can't find a job because of the job market or because you have a criminal record, don't think that it's a bad thing because chances are, no employer is ever going to give you enough money for you to live comfortably for a long period of time. They'll give you just enough to keep you coming back every two weeks. Take it as a sign that the universe is saying that this may be the best time to create your own job by starting your own business. (By the way...If you do have a record, you can always see if you are eligible to have it expunged or deleted, or see if you can change your name legally and get a fresh start).

If you don't have to have a lot of money to start taking steps to open your own business, in every city there are employment centers where you have the free use of services such as the Internet, phones, printers, copy machines and fax machines. Some are called Work Force, Work Source and Zu Can Centers. You can design your business cards, print your new flyers for your new business or even start building your website right from these free resource locations. Before you run out and spend money to register your business, at least get your business cards, get your website up and running and start doing some word of mouth promoting. Because as you get feedback from your potential customers you may find out you'd rather work in another field or even change the name of your business. VistaPrint.com has inexpensive business cards and Wix.com is a platform where you can easily build your own website for free. As far as promoting, you can start with friends and family members, your followers on your social sites and simply by posting flyers in your neighborhood. You can also sign up with companies that will keep you informed of networking events for free or for a small fee. Or speak to the SBA (Small Business Association) in your area to see if they know of any networking events where you can promote your business.

2. INVESTING

LESSON 64: The best investment you can make is in yourself

- Traditional forms of investing.

Sometimes they invest in startup companies and get a percentage of all the revenue that the company brings in once it is up and running.

Sometimes they live off of "Interest income" which is what you would expect interest earned on money invested in bonds, CDs and savings accounts.

A bond is a debt investment in which an investor loans money to an entity such as a corporation or government, which borrows the money for a fixed period of time for a fixed or variable interest rate. Though bonds usually have a low interest rate they are one of the less risky forms of investments.

A CD has fixed interest rate, can be issued in any denomination and has a certain maturity date, which usually ranges from one month to five years and are usually issued at banks. Usually the longer the term of the CD, the higher return you'll get on your money.

Most people are familiar with a savings account, which is a bank account that earns interest. Because the interest rate on regular savings account is so low, in order to be able to live off of that interest you'd have to have millions in the bank.

Sometimes Investment income can also be generated as a "capital gain", or the profit from the sale of an asset, such as stock or real estate.
"Dividends" are a distribution of a company's profits that can be earned by investing in such assets as

stocks and mutual funds.

Sometimes they "play the stock market". Some traders are "day traders" (they'll buy and sell stock within a day or two) and some investors "buy and hold" the stock for months or often years. Technically speaking, whether a "day trading" or "buying and holding', anyone who buys shares of stock becomes a part owner in the company that they buy stocks in. This gives them the right to vote at shareholders' meetings and it permits them to receive profits (dividends) from the company. (The stock market is one of the riskier types of investments).

If you don't have much money but are ready to test the stock market, consider trading "penny stocks", (look for stocks that only cost a few pennies). Though I can't tell you to invest in any specific companies, I would say pay special attention to technology, and pharmaceutical companies, especially those that deal with medicinal marijuana. From my understanding two states have already legalized the use of medical marijuana, and I can only assume that more states will follow in the future.

I don't think most people realize how easy it is to start trading stock. The words "stock market" used to sound so intimidating to me before I knew how it all worked. I thought that I had to have thousands and thousands of dollars to start and I also thought that I had to have a fund manager to manage all those thousands. Not true. When I finally tried my hand in the stock market it was with a modest forty dollars on TDAmeritrade.com. On sites like that one, as well as Fidelity.com, Vanguard and ETrade.com you can transfer money from your checking account within a day or two, look up the "ticker symbol" for the company in which you want to invest and buy shares without a fund manager. All the sites I mentioned have customer service reps you can call to guide you through your purchase.

Another form of traditional investing is mutual funds. This is a mixture of different stocks, and most people consider this a form of *diversification* to lessen the risks of buying stocks. (However, if the whole stock market crashes and you only have your money invested in mutual funds it doesn't matter how much you spread it out, you're going to lose your money).

To truly diversify you'd need a good mixture of the four asset classes.

Owning businesses that create cash flow.

Owning investment real estate that is creating cash flow.

Trading paper assets (such as stocks, currencies, bonds, money & market accounts).

The textbook definition of "Hedging" is an investment to limit the risk of another investment. Insurance is an example of real-world hedging. For example, you can hedge again against the stock market with commodities, such as silver, gold and oil. Which is basically holding on to tangible valuables as a form of insurance that you can cash in in any market.

A great percentage of the successful accumulate their wealth by buying real estate. They make money buy purchasing homes and renting them out or by purchasing homes that need major repairing. After they rehabilitate the houses they sell them for way more than they bought them for, or simply by buying homes below value and selling them for a profit.

3. CREATING PASSIVE & RESIDUAL INCOME

Active income or linear income is income that comes from the direct result of your labor. The most common example is an "hourly wage", which means you're only getting paid for each hour that you are actively working; so your income is limited because after all, there are only 24 hours in a day.

There are a lot people who get paid huge amounts of money to become the CEO of a company, play sports, or to star in TV shows or movies. However, to excel in these positions and make top dollar requires a tremendous amount lot of hard work and requires a level of dedication and discipline that most people lack...and even if you master the dedication and discipline you still have to show up to work to earn that money.

People often get **passive** and **residual** income confused. **Passive income** comes from business investments in which the individual is not actively involved. For example, income from rental property revenue, dividend stock payments, website revenue and money generated from machines.

DIFFERENT TYPES OF PASSIVE INCOME

...Or what I refer to as Non-Traditional ways of investing.

Real Estate is one of the steadiest forms of residual income. People will always need shelter. You don't have to be the person doing the maintenance and collecting the rent either. You can hire a property manager to run the units and in most cases they charge as little as 10%.

You don't always have to *own* property to make residual rental income either. If you have a spare room in your apartment you can rent it out for a monthly fee.

Invest in bonds or the stock market.

Annuities are a fixed sum of money paid to someone each year. It's a form of insurance or investment entitling the investor to a series of annual sums. They sometimes come in the form of insurance products that you pay for but then can provide you passive income in form of monthly payments for life.

Affiliate Marketing. You can form partnerships with other companies, put their product on your website and receive a commission on each product that is sold. Google AdSense is a great platform to start on.

If you sell items on a website and you have a distribution company that is processing payments and fulfilling the orders, that's also a form of passive income.

If you only have a few hundred or a few thousand dollars as startup capital, then machines such as ATM machines, soda machines, snack machines, candy machines, toy machines, video game machines, weight machines, breathalyzer machines, filtered water machines, even photo booths and pool tables are a good way to make passive income. If you can secure great locations they can generate great income. For example, if you own an ATM that charges $3 per transaction, and you get 50 transactions per day, you can make $150 a day (which is $4500 a month).

If you have a large lump sum of money to start with, then car washes and Laundromats are also a great source of passive income.

Residual income is income you get when you continue to get paid after the work is finished. This includes royalties from books, movies, or songs and even income that comes from a business or from renting real estate. It's income that comes from creating an asset that continues to pay you after the work has been completed.

DIFFERENT TYPES OF RESIDUAL INCOME

You can get residual income from:

The sales of a book you wrote. Authors get royalties each month from hardcover, paperback and electronic books like the Kindle.

Audiobooks are a form of residual income. They're sold on ITunes, on audible.com and sold from .99 cents to $9.99 for each download.

Voice over work. You don't even have to be the author of any book, you can simply record your voice while reading someone's book and upload it to Audible.com and get half of the sales each time that audio book is purchased.

Music is a form of residual income and it's easier than ever to sell your music online today through platforms like ITunes and Google Play.

You don't have to be able to sing to make music. If you are great at composing or producing music you can sell instrumentals.

You can license your music and earn a royalty off of your music when someone chooses to use it. Music is often licensed for YouTube Videos, commercials, and more.

You can sell Information in the form of audio files. Perhaps you're knowledgeable at something, but you don't have enough info to create an entire audio book. You can create shorter mp3 files full of useful information and sell them for .99 cents each.

Make a video course. We are all experts at something! It may not be math but it may be cooking or babysitting or painting. Create your own video course and upload it to Udemy.com, WebinarFusionPro.com, Kajabi.com or Fedora.com so that users can purchase it. This is a great choice if you are very knowledgeable about a particular subject.

If you know how to build Apps you can sell them on ITunes and on Google Play.

Sell Stock Photos. If you're good at photography there are plenty of websites that you can showcase your work on and people will pay a fee for the right to use your images.

If you're good at graphic design you can design T-shirts and sell them on Cafe Press and other similar sites that allow users to make custom design items like T-shirts. Every time someone purchases one of your items, you get paid!

If you are good at graphic design you can also sell digital files on Etsy and other similar platforms; Every time someone chooses your design you get paid.

Network Marketing (also called multi-level marketing) can be a way of making passive income. Coffee, teas, supplements and beauty products seem to be the products of choice. Companies such as Young Living Oils, Avon and Mary Kay are examples of network marketing companies. After you've built your sales team you can earn passive income from everyone they sign up who sells things *for* the company or purchase things *from* the company. Be careful with this option though; make sure it's a long standing reputable company and not some fly-by-night scheme though. If you aren't selling great products that you'd actually use yourself, if you aren't a people person and if you are uncomfortable with sales, I can guarantee that you will not be successful at network marketing.

FUNDING YOUR DREAM

LESSON 65: You don't have to have money to make money. You can barter.

When it comes time to fund your dream you may feel stuck if you don't have startup capital. But keep in mind that you don't always have to have money to make money...if you think creatively. Learn to embrace "partnering and bartering" and also seek out organizations, associations and groups like those on MeetUp.com with the same philosophy.

THE POWER OF BARTERING

The first thing you need to do is create a *wish list* of all things that you need in order to reach your goals. Then go through your address book and write down everyone who can help you to get those things or who can help you to get those tasks done. Then you need to work up the nerve and call them. Perhaps you need a website and you have the contact information for someone who builds websites for a living. You may not be able to pay him in dollars but perhaps you can pay him with time by assisting him with something he needs help with or by offering him products or a service that you or your company offer. (If not for free, then discounted). You may be able to house sit, pet sit, baby sit or run his errands for a week in exchange for a website. Perhaps you can even pay him a percentage of each item you sell on the website for the first six months. Or perhaps you can refer three paying customers to him so he can build their websites. *Put on your thinking cap, it's time to get creative.*

Perhaps you can pitch an idea to someone who has office space for lease. If you don't have the money upfront see if you can draw up a contract where you use the space for the first six months and pay him a percentage of what the business makes until things start gaining traction (the space is empty anyway, what will he have to lose?)

Perhaps you want to start a babysitting service in your home but it's too small; perhaps you can ask a family member to use their house everyday while they're at work and you spilt what you earn with them.

Perhaps you bake amazing cakes but don't have the capital to start your own bakery, maybe you can ask a few local restaurants that don't sell those kind of cakes to sell them in their space and you split the profits.

You can also work on your credit and apply for a business loan.

There may be business incubators. Business incubators are organizations that help new and startup companies to develop by offering services like office space and management training. They usually have resources to help you build your business and can sometimes offer referrals to assist you get funding. Also subscribe to AllBusiness.com and NBIA.org (National Business Incubator Association) are great websites. NBIA is a diverse group made up of industry professionals who help guide, support and develop entrepreneurs worldwide. It strives to further enhance the global entrepreneurial ecosystem by providing thought leadership; education, resources and networking to assist members to better serve the entrepreneurs in their communities and regions.

If you're working a job that you hate I'd love to tell you to put in your two weeks notice or quit immediately...but that wouldn't be the wisest decision without first planning your exit strategy! Give yourself six months, or a year, or even two years if you need more time...but put a date on paper. Write down a date by when you want to leave and also write down a certain amount that you want to have saved when you do leave. Writing it down on paper and setting a deadline creates accountability.

I've interviewed many successful people to find out how they started on their wealth path and almost half of them said that they used the money they saved from their corporate job to fund their first business venture. One of those people was Randy Hazelton a serial entrepreneur; An African American young man in his thirties who is now part owner in twelve successful restaurants in the Atlanta area.

When it's time to step out on faith and start your own business, the best position to be in is to have some money already saved up. If you have no money, are unemployed, between jobs or can't find a job, the good news is that you're in the second best position to start pursuing what it is that you really want to do...look at the upside...you have all the time in the world. Before you rush out and hop right back in a job just so you can pay your bills, try eliminating the bills for a while so you can work on your dreams. If you are near the end of your lease perhaps you can put your belongings in storage and stay with your family or friends for a while. That may not be an exciting idea, but remember why you're doing it.

COMFORT KILLS MORE DREAMS THAN FAILURE

A close friend of mine always talked about working for himself someday. He absolutely hated the job that he was in; it seemed like there was no way out. Then after four years of working for the company they fired him. He felt devastated. Though he made great money and had some savings he still felt like he didn't have enough saved to start the specific business venture that he had in mind. Then a few days after they let him go he found out that they were giving him a severance package. This was it! He finally had enough to start his business! Probably not enough to build his whole empire but he had enough to make the first step! I was so excited for him! I wrote him a long email telling him that that day was the start of his new life. He finally had the time to read about the business he wanted to start and do his research and due diligence. And you know what he did? He immediately started sending out his resume to companies similar to the one he previously worked for and in less than a week he was hired. He quickly resorted back to what was the most comfortable for him...working. Not what he wanted to do in his heart...not what would make him most happy...but what was sadly comfortable.

TO BE...OR NOT TO BE

I thought that everyone had a dream of becoming an entrepreneur, working for themselves, starting their dream business, making their own schedule and being free from the constraints of a job one day. I learned differently when I had an in-depth coaching session with a woman by the name of Denisha. I was giving her all this advice about how to start her own business, put together a business plan and find her ideal clients, and finally she said "That's too much work and way too risky. She said "I just want to go to school, get a degree, work in a nice office and have a steady paycheck coming in that's enough for me to not only pay my bills but go shopping every once in a while".

After that conversation I realized that my dream isn't the same as everyone else's, which isn't a good or a bad things because it's all a matter of preference. After all…if everyone were a boss then there would be no workers; and being a boss is a very big job. Not only do you depend on your direct effort in order to eat, but your employees do as well…and that's a lot of responsibility. Everyone isn't cut out for that type of pressure. You must make the personal decision to be …or not to be an entrepreneur for yourself, because you alone will have to live with it. If you've made the personal decision to work for someone else instead of working for yourself remember the following lesson:

LESSON 66: Never work for a paycheck alone, but work to build relationships

NEVER WORK FOR A PAYCHECK

Many people work for huge companies that have hundreds or thousands of people that they do business with and when that company downsizes, or closes down completely, the employees have to find a new job and start all over from scratch because they have none of the client's contacts info or haven't formed any personal bond or relationships with those clients. That is *not* working smart. Never assume that your position with a company is permanent, no matter how good the pay is and how valuable you feel to them. Always plan ahead. You can plan ahead by building your own client list, make a few notes about each client you accumulate; it can be something as small as a reminder of their birthday so you can call or send an email, or even drop them a card in the mail. It may be a small gesture on your part, but it may be huge to them. Or if your kids are the same age as their kids perhaps you can suggest that you schedule a play date together. Even if your schedules may never allow, just the fact that you offered that invitation may be the difference between you starting from the ground up or having clients already line up (if you were to get laid off, go to another company or even chose to start your own business in a similar field later). Even if you think you wouldn't ever need to do business with those clients in the future, it's best to have those relationships and not need them, rather than to need them in the future and not have them.

LESSON 67: Never work just for the paycheck, work to build a network.

If you have to work for someone then choose a job that gives you more than just income. Choose one that gives you the opportunity to network with a class of people you otherwise wouldn't have met. Choose one that offers employee discounts on their products or services; and not just any product or service but make sure it's one that you already use, and use often. Perhaps you'd consider working for your cell phone provider, or the dealership where you plan on purchasing a car from in the future, or even the apartment complex that you live in; that way you'd get the discount off of a bill that you already have to pay regardless.

FLEXIBILITY WHILE FUNDING YOUR DREAM

The ideal plan would be to fund your dream without the constraints of working a traditional nine-to-five. I love the direction society is moving in today because now more than ever, there are many flexible options to do so.

For example, there are a lot of legitimate work-from-home opportunities, no sales just simple customer service. You don't have to commute, you don't have to put gas in your car, and you don't even have to get dressed! Arise.com is one of those work-from-home companies that are always looking customer service representatives in the United States, United Kingdom and Canada to fill positions from reputable companies like Apple, AT&T and Disney Cruise Lines.

If you have a car you can be driver for Uber or Lyft and work as little or as many hours as you want.

If you have a second car, or don't use your car full-time because you travel a lot or you live close to work, you can rent it out by the day, week or month on RelayRides.com.

If you have an extra room in your apartment, you can rent it out on AirBandB.com.

I love how society is slowly putting the power in the hands of the people. I'm sure there are more flexible ways out there to earn money that doesn't include working a nine-to-five, so start researching options on the Internet.

If you do work in the corporate world, don't hesitate to utilize Corporate America capital to fund your passion or your business. So, before you get frustrated and quit your job, formulate a plan. Each paycheck put aside a fixed amount of money towards one specific thing that will get you closer to your goal. Before you just up and quit, think things through, because in a lot of states you will not be eligible to collect unemployment benefits if you were the one who left the company willingly.

"The best way to help the poor is to not be one of them"

4. Don't lend money.

You are not in the business of lending; you are not Bank of America! You have to be totally fine with saying "no". Your savings cushion can't get plush enough for you to start investing if you keep dipping into it. If you create a reputation of bailing out your friends and family whenever they come running...then you'll forever be the one they come running to. And as long as you're their "bail man" then you'll never be able to reach YOUR financial goals. If you do decide to lend out money don't expect to get it back. I've seen many friendships and relationships turn sour when it was time to repay a loan and the lender couldn't or simply didn't want to repay it.

I remember a friend asked me to borrow some money, the first time I loaned it to him without hesitation. But then I started to see a pattern in him borrowing money from me. So the next time he needed a loan, I told him that I can lend it to him but I have to pawn something first and they'd charge me 20% interest so he'd have to pay that back. It was shocking how fast he changed his mind and told me that was okay, I didn't have to go out of my way and that he'd find another solution. I was relieved! Though I highly advise you against it, if you do decide to lend out money ask for collateral (in case they aren't willing or able to pay you back) or charge interest because that money could have been earning you interest elsewhere.

"The rich collect assets; the poor collect liabilities...and the middle class buy liabilities that they think are assets".   — Rich Dad Poor Dad

5. Collect assets, not liabilities

An asset is anything that increases in value or generates income; basically, an asset is anything that will put money into your pocket (like gold, silver, art, antiques, land, real-estate, celebrity memorabilia or even a book, movie or song that you're earning royalties from).

A liability is anything that takes money out of your pocket. (Like money spent that only puts you in debt like a car that you took out an auto loan to get). Most people consider a home and car assets, but technically if you aren't generating money off of them they're not assets.

So before purchasing something that you've been tempted to buy, ask yourself if it's an asset or liability, is it taking you closer or further from your financial goal?

If it's taking you further away then don't get it. Once you get to the point where you have your assets and investments bringing in enough money monthly, then feel free to splurge on all the luxuries you desire. The greatest thing of all is that in the process of saving, investing, building assets and becoming wealth conscious, you'll become conscious...period. Now wiser and self-assured you'll realize that half of the "luxuries" that you wanted no longer be appeal to you. You'll realize that the biggest reason why you wanted most of those things were to keep up with other people, who you now realize weren't able to afford those things in the first place because they were using *debt* to finance their lifestyle!

6. Take advantage of compound interest

"Compound interest is the eighth wonder of the world. He who understands it, earns it; he who doesn't, pays it".   *— Albert Einstein*

Compound interest is calculated on the original principal as well as on the interest that is gained from the previous periods of a deposit. Think of compound interest as "interest on top of interest". It makes your investment grow more rapidly than simple interest, because simple interest is only calculated on the original principal. To help you understand compound interest better, I took the following example from basic-mathematics.com

If 4000 dollars is deposited into a bank account and the annual interest rate is 8%.

How much is the interest after 4 years?

Use the following simple interest formula:
$I = p \times r \times t$

(p) is the principal or money deposited, (r) is the rate of interest and (t) is time. We get:

$I = p \times r \times t$

$I = 4000 \times 8\% \times 4$

$I = 4000 \times 0.08 \times 4$

$I = 1280$ dollars

However, compound interest is the interest earned not only on the original principal, but also on all interests earned previously.

In other words, at the end of each year, the interest earned is added to the original amount and the money is reinvested.

If we use compound interest for the situation above, the interest will be computed as follow:

Interest at the end of the first year:

$I = 4000 \times 0.08 \times 1$

$I = 320$ dollars

Your new principal per say is now $4000 + 320 = 4320$

Interest at the end of the second year:

$I = 4320 \times 0.08 \times 1$
$I = 345.6$ dollars

Your new principal is now $4320 + 345.6 = 4665.6$
Interest at the end of the third year:
$I = 4665.6 \times 0.08 \times 1$

$I = 373.248$ dollars

Your new principal is now $4665.6 + 373.248 = 5038.848$

Interest at the end of the fourth year:
$I = 5038.848 \times 0.08 \times 1$

I = 403.10784 dollars

Your new principal is now 5038.848 + 403.10784 = 5441.95584

Total interest earned = 5441.95584 − 4000 = 1441.95584

The difference in money between compound interest and simple interest is 1441.96 - 1280 = 161.96

As you see...compound interest produces more favorable results for you. The longer you leave your money, the more powerful the compound interest effect. So the earlier you start saving, is the better...(as long as you're not withdrawing the interest being accrued). Compound interest also applies to debt, but not in a good way, because the longer you leave a debt unpaid, the debt will continually increase.

I hope that helps you to grasp the concept of compound interest better. If you're having trouble understanding it, the most important thing you need to know when it's time for you to invest...is to ask your bank if they're using "compound interest" and if they do, then take advantage of those accounts that offer it.

7. Maximize Your Taxes

In America, taxes are one of most people's biggest expenses. You'll never be free from them. As long as you live you'll have to pay taxes...and if you don't then Uncle Sam will take you down like a linebacker. I believe in the tax system, however, I also realize that many people don't take advantage of their tax benefits and deductions simply because they don't know about them. Some of the most overlooked deductions include daycare costs, items donated to organizations, and 'junk cars' given away. Did you know that if you are self-employed you can write off a portion of your cell phone bill, a portion of the cost of your computer, a part of the rent you pay, some of your utilities, and even mileage and gas used for your car if you often use your vehicle for business use?

The more ways you can find to save on taxes *legally*, is the more money you'll have to save & then to ultimately invest. When I asked my financial advisor what were some ways to save on taxes he jokingly responded, "Buy a house, start a business and have a baby". Yes, those are the three biggest ways that most people can receive some of their money back, but those aren't the only ways.

The first thing you should do is Consult a Tax professional.

Then read some books on taxes to see if there are ways you can save or maximize your tax deductions. One book I found handy that pointed out a lot of things that were tax deductible was "Deduct It".

You should check if you qualify for the earned income tax credit. You can get back credited as much as $6,000 if you earn less than $50,000.

Consider starting that business that you always wanted to start.

Being a business owner can also help your tax situation because entrepreneurs have better control over how they pay taxes. They have the choice of keeping more money in their company instead of taking it out as income, (income which they are taxed on).

If you are a parent of a child under 18, there are multiple credits that you are eligible for, including credit for childcare costs.

If you are divorced know that alimony payments are tax deductible.

Single parents sometimes forget to claim head of household status, which allows certain tax advantages, including the ability to claim dependents.

If you have children that you plan on sending to

college one day, consider creating a 529-college savings account. Whatever you save in that account will grow tax-free as long as the money goes toward tuition.

After most people pay off their credit card debt, auto loan and student loans, naturally, they want to pay off their mortgage. That may not be the best option for everybody though. Mortgage interest payments are tax deductible, which means homeowners benefit, from a tax perspective, by keeping their mortgage for as long as possible. Though you'll be incurring more interest payments, you can actually come out ahead if you put the money that you would have used to pay off your mortgage in an account that was incurring more interest each month than what you're paying on your mortgage. In my last finance workshop, one of my business associates, who is a financial advisor pointed out that paying off your mortgage as quickly as possible isn't always your best option for everyone for two reasons.

1. If you pay off your home and decide to sell it one day but the housing market is down and the house is valued for half of what you bought it for...then what? *You just lost half of your money.*

2. If you made all your payments on time but lose your job and you decide to take out a loan against your

house that's paid off; even if you have an 800 credit score no bank will lend you any money because...you don't have a J.O.B.

There are two benefits to voluntarily lowering your take-home paycheck by increasing your retirement. First, you increase your retirement savings (that's great because it's way easier to make more money when you you're young), and second, you lower your tax liability because money deposited into certain retirement accounts is tax deductible.

In addition to tax-deductible gifts, individuals can also receive up to $13,000 without paying taxes. Parents can even join forces to give each child $26,000 with a technique dubbed "gift splitting."

Keep all your receipts and track all your expenses, especially medical expenses, because certain health-related expenses, like acupuncture, bandages, and breast pumps are tax deductible. There is a list of eligible items, visit irs.gov.

Make your home more energy efficient and you'll receive credits for a number of things like installing insulation, solar panels, new windows or doors, and getting a qualified heating and cooling system.

If you have things around the house that you don't need, instead of throwing them out or giving them to random people, donate them to Goodwill and write it off as a tax deduction.

Also, ordinary losses on the sale of stock can be deducted as capital losses, which can offset capital gains.

These are just some ways you can maximize your tax deductions. Tax debt is one debt that you don't want to ignore…at all. It *will* land you in jail! If you find that you owe taxes and can't afford to pay the whole amount ask for an extension, or ask to be put on some form of a payment plan or installment plan. In some cases you can apply to offer a compromise in order to settle your bill for less than you actually owe. Offers in compromise is a fancy name for "negotiation" and they are awarded based on your ability to pay, your income and your expenses.

CREATIVELY RAISING CAPITAL

This is the time to start thinking creatively and operating way outside of the box!

With platforms such as GoFundMe.com and KickStarter.com raising money from family and friends have become easier. With crowd-funding sites like these two, it's easy to link to your social sites and publicly share the amount you are raising and why you are raising the money. You can also effortlessly include photos and videos to better tell your story.

Crowd lending or (Peer to Peer lending P2PL) is the practice of lending money to unrelated individuals, without going through a traditional financial institution such as a bank.

- Lending Club is one of the world's largest online marketplace connecting borrowers and investors. Their goal is to transform the banking system to make credit more affordable and investing more rewarding. They operate at a lower cost than traditional bank lending programs and pass the savings on to borrowers in the form of lower rates and to investors in the form of solid returns.

- Prosper is also a peer-to-peer company and is a popular alternative to traditional loans and investing options. They cut out the middleman to connect people who need money with those who have money to invest.

Have a fundraiser! The location can be your front yard. You can rent bouncy house on a perfect summer weekend and turn your front hard into a kiddy park. You can have slip and slides, balloons, face painting and serve snacks and lemonade; and just encourage neighborhood parents to make donations.

Have a yard sale or sell the things you don't need on eBay or Craigslist.

On Craigslist there is section for "free things. Most of those things are in good condition but the people may be moving and don't have a truck to take those things with them or may not have the extra space to store them. What's one's man's trash is another man's treasure. You can rent a storage unit, (or store them in your garage or spare room if you have one), pick up those items, and take photos of them and post them right back up on craigslist but for a fee this time around.

If some of those free things from Craigslist aren't in a good enough condition to sell but they are made of metal; then instead of listing them for sale, you can take them to a recycling center that buys scrap metal.

If you're a teen or have a teenage child who is looking to make some extra income you can sell soda cans. You don't have to collect them one by one but you can talk to some local businesses, churches and schools in your community, and ask them to put all their empty cans in a designated area and you can schedule one day a week to do the pick ups and then sell them to a recycling center that buys aluminum.

My niece Sheri and sister Danielle, were thirteen at the time, they came to me for ideas on how they could make money since they weren't old enough to get a regular job yet. When I gave them the idea of turning in cans and scrap metal for money, Sheri clearly said she wasn't going to do that and Danielle just stayed silent. To my surprise, I was shocked when I visited only a few weeks later and Danielle's house was filled with bags and bags of industrial sized trash bags full of cans!

Danielle went for it and she was all in! She partnered with her church and had been working diligently collecting the cans. You should have seen the size of the smile on her face when she cashed in those cans for cold hard cash. It wasn't a lot of money but it was a start. But most importantly I knew she was on the success track because she was willing to do what others weren't!

You can participate in clinical studies. Some of them require healthy participants and others require participants to have certain pre-existing conditions. So if you have any pre-existing conditions and no insurance, this may be a chance to get free cutting edge treatment *and* get paid at the same time.

You can sell plasma…yes blood; and earn up to $300 a month doing so.

For more creative ways to make money check out my videos on Youtube.com/BajeFletcher

LIST OF BUSINESS & FINANCE MAGAZINES

Bloomberg,

Entrepreneur,

Fast Company,

Financial Planning,

Forbes,

Harvard Business Review,

Home Business,

INC, Direct Marketing,

Investor's Business Daily,

Money, Kiplinger's,

Moneywise, Economist,

Small Business Opportunities,

The Economist,

US Banker Barron's, Fortune,

Wired

All of the magazines I mentioned have great daily articles so subscribe to all of their websites.

A few years ago I met a very wealthy friend for lunch. He suggested we dine at a private "members only" business club to which he belonged. It was located on the very top floor of one of the high-rises in a major city. On the way out my eyes caught a stack of magazines. Being an avid reader, I grabbed a copy as I left. Prior to this day I never heard of this particular publication. It was called "Worth Magazine" Feel free to subscribe to the list of magazines I previously mentioned for *"information"*, however, for *"inspiration"*, get a copy of "Worth" magazine! That's if you can get your hands on it. As I flipped through the pages and read the titles of the articles, I quickly realized that this was no ordinary finance periodical. "Do you need to rethink your estate planning?", "How can I best prepare for the challenges that may come with sudden wealth?", "Do I need a ransom policy?", were just a few of the headlines. This was clearly exclusively for a certain income bracket...millionaires and beyond. Worth is an American financial, lifestyle and wealth management magazine. It tackles financial, lifestyle and legal issues for high-net-worth individuals and features stories about innovative wealth creators and provides expert advice on investing and wealth management. It's mailed six times a year to individuals listed on a database of high-net-worth households in major markets, including: the New York metropolitan area, Fairfield County, the Delaware Valley, Boston, Chicago, South Florida, Dallas, Houston, San Francisco, Los Angeles and Orange County. The good news is that magazine is also available on some newsstands; you just have to locate which ones. Hopefully it will open up your appetite for success by showing you that there is a whole other wealthy world out there. In the meantime check out Worth.com.

LIST OF FINANCE BOOKS

Automatic Millionaire
Cash Flow Quadrant
Financial Peace
How Rich People Think
Intelligent Investor
Law of Success
Money, Master The Game
Retire Overseas
Retire Young, Retire Rich
Rich Dad Poor Dad
Rich Habits
The Richest Man in Babylon
Secrets of a Millionaire's Mind
Smart Money, Smart Kids
The 4-Hour Workweek
The 8-Hour Workweek
The 50th Law
The ABC's of Real Estate Investing
The Answer
The Cash Flow Quadrant
The Courage to be Rich
The Divine Law of Compensation
The Idiot's Guide to Improving Your Credit Score

The Millionaire Fast Lane
The Millionaire Handbook
The Millionaire Next Door
The Richest Man in Babylon
The Science of Getting Rich
The Wealth Choice
The Wealth Cure
Think and Grow Rich
Total Money Makeover
Why We Want You to be Rich
Young Fabulous and Broke

Rich Dad, Poor Dad's board game "Cash Flow 101" is also an excellent way to learn about money. In your search for wealth and while investing in yourself try not to break the bank on books, software or subscriptions; instead round up a few of your friends and make your own little "wealth club". Perhaps one of you could get a membership to a finance site but share the login and password with the group, or perhaps each of you can buy a different book and rotate the books among members. Or perhaps each of you can subscribe to a specific magazine and swap it out with someone else in the group once you're finished. I challenge you to be conservative and creative.

JOIN THE NEW RICH!

"The New Rich" is a term coined by Tim Ferris in his book "The 4-Hour Work Week" which simply means people escaped the bondage of a nine-to-five and live the lives they want, by working from home or a remote location. People who make money while they sleep, and live like they're retired now!

- Benefits of Doing Business in The Cyber Age

Technology has made almost everything easier and so convenient. Because of technology, with each passing day there are fewer and fewer reasons why anyone has to leave their house.

You can shop online and choose same day or one-day shipping & FedEx will deliver it right to your doorstep

With apps like "Uber Eats" you can have food from your favorite restaurant delivered,

You can have a grocery delivery service pick up the things off of your grocery list from your local supermarket and bring them to your house,

Even some liquor stores deliver alcohol,

No more long lines! You can renew your driver's license online,

You can earn a college degree right from the comfort of your own home,

If you can get hired by a top company like Apple or AT&T to work for them from home,

...*So why not run your own business from your own home?*

In this day and time, unless you render some sort of physical service there is really no need to have a physical office or to work out of an actual commercial building. A lot of very successful businesses are now run from homes i.e. "Home offices", "satellite offices", "remote locations", or from down the block at the "cyber café"...and even "plain ole' coffee shop". So as long as you have a reliable laptop and an Internet connection, you can market and sell just about anything, to just about anyone from just about anywhere in the world! Isn't that amazing?

With so many companies offering "print on demand" or "manufacture on demand" services you no longer need lots of physical space to store inventory. You can just use a printer or manufacturing company that does orders "on demand", so you don't have to have them make or ship anything until *after* a customer places an order with you. If you're in a line of business where you absolutely have to have storage space, you can consider renting space in a storage facility close to your home, for a fraction of what it would take to lease a commercial building.

There is much money to be made in the cyber age. Put a pen to paper and think of a product or service you can offer the world. You don't even have to create an "original" product or service. Even if it's something that is already in existence, if you can figure out a way to make it more convenient for consumers to access, then you too can come out on top.

Chapter 9

How To Get What You Want

HOW TO GET WHAT YOU WANT

The first step to getting what you want is asking yourself a series of questions, then taking some time in a quiet place to reflect, while you answer those questions honestly.

On a scale of 1-10 how happy are you with your life?

_____

What would make your life a 9 or 10 if it's not?

_____
_____
_____
_____

What does your ideal life look like?

_____
_____
_____
_____
_____

What do you think has been stopping you from achieving your idea life?

_____
_____
_____

What are some things you need in order to live your ideal life? (E.g. resources, referrals or financing)

_____

_____

_____

_____

Who are some people you need to meet, learn from or partner with in order to live your ideal life?

_____

_____

_____

_____

What are some things you can start doing now so you can start living your ideal life?

_____

_____

_____

What are some beliefs, habits or relationships you need to discontinue in order for you to live the life you want?

_____

_____

_____

_____

_____

_____

What kind of person do you want to be?

_____

_____

_____

_____

What do you have to do to become that person?

_____

_____

_____

_____

What are some steps you can start taking today towards becoming your future self?

_____

_____

_____

_____

What motivates you?

_____

_____

_____

_____

Who inspires you and why?

_____

_____

_____

What are you passionate about?

_____

_____

_____

_____

What are some ways that you can make money off of
your passion?

_____

_____

_____

_____

What are some things that you are good at?

_____

_____

_____

_____

Out of all of those things, what is the ONE that you're
best at?

_____

_____

_____

_____

_____

_____

_____

_____

What are some ways you can make money off of that one thing?

_____

_____

_____

_____

If you're not sure about your passion or talents, what are some new activities you are willing to try until you find your passion & talents?

_____

_____

_____

Have you ever had and idea for a new product or service?

_____

What type of people you think could benefit from your product or service?

_____

_____

_____

_____

_____

_____

_____

_____

_____

Where do you think you can find those people so you can market that product or service to them?

_____
_____
_____
_____

Who do you personally know that you can call to be your first customers?

_____
_____
_____
_____

How much would it take to bring that idea to life?

_____
_____
_____
_____

What are some things you can do to come up with that money?

_____
_____

Who would you need to help you make this a success?

_____
_____
_____

Are there any skills you need that you don't already have to make this idea a reality? If so, what are they?

_____

_____

_____

_____

What kind of workshops or seminars can you attend, what kind of books can you read or who can you partner with to acquire those skills?

_____

_____

_____

_____

If those skills are too time consuming to learn, who are some people that already posses those skills so you can partner with them?

_____

_____

_____

_____

Where do you want to be in 1-2 years?

_____

_____

_____

_____

Where do you want to be in 5-10 years?

_____

_____

_____

What age do you want to retire by? (How much money
do you want to have when you retire? And how much
would you have to earn each year in order to reach that
goal?)

_____

_____

_____

How will you deal with obstacles that you'll face?

_____

_____

_____

_____

What are some measures you'll take so you won't get
distracted?

_____

_____

_____

_____

_____

_____

_____

_____

Who will you call for support when you feel overwhelmed?

_____

_____

_____

_____

If today was your last day on earth, what would you have regret not doing?

_____

_____

_____

_____

What are the things on your bucket list?

_____

_____

_____

_____

_____

_____

_____

_____

_____

_____

_____

_____

_____

GOAL CATEGORIES

The more detailed you can get with your goals is the better your chances you'll have at achieving them. Here are eight of the most common goal categories for you to tackle.

What are your relationship goals & deadline?

_____

_____

_____

_____

What are your educational or career goals & deadline?

_____

_____

_____

_____

What are your financial goals & deadline?

_____

_____

_____

_____

What are your health, & fitness goals & deadline?

_____

_____

_____

What are your personal development goals? (E.g. intellectual & emotional)

_____

_____

_____

_____

What are your quality of life goals (E.g. leisure travel, material, friends & fun)?

_____

_____

_____

_____

What are your spiritual goals? (Note that spirituality doesn't necessarily mean religious)

_____

_____

_____

_____

What are your contribution goals (How do you want to give back to society)? E.g. fostering / adopting a child, starting a non-profit, donating money or volunteering your time to causes close to your heart.

_____

_____

_____

_____

Finally, ask yourself what do you have to do in each category, each day, in order to achieve these goals? Write those answers on a sheet of paper or purchase the companion workbook to this book called "Why I am successful now!" to help you keep track of your daily tasks and goals.

This chapter is to help you identify your goals, get your goals out of your head and on paper so that you can easily refer to them daily. There will be times when you lose focus or get distracted. There will be times when you sway off course, there will be days when you feel uninspired, and your goals seem far fetched, and those are the days you will need to look over these pages the most, so keep this book handy.

Reading this book alone will get you nowhere, you have to actually apply yourself by taking action now and making a commitment to yourself that you are going to put these lessons into practice immediately. Answer ALL the questions in this chapter *right now* and start creating your goal board today...your success depends on it!

Chapter 10

How to Thrive in Their System

HOW TO THRIVE IN THEIR SYSTEM

We live in a system that is set up in a way that most people barely get by. They educate us just enough to show us how to be good workers...for them. After all, the less we know is the more they can capitalize on us. They pay us just enough to pay our bills, they pay us only a small fraction of what we bring in for their company, and to add insult to injury, they pay us two weeks after we earned our hard earned money. They give us lines of credit without first telling us how credit works. No wonder why most people are waist up in debt! My goal for you, is to not only "survive in the system", but thrive in the system. Just because you weren't born with a good hands of card doesn't mean that you're doomed to fail. You just have to know how to play the hands you are dealt. You can win at their game, but you must first learn the rules. And that's what this book teaches!

SETTING & EXCEEDING YOUR FINANCIAL GOALS

A lot of people come to me with questions about money; how to make it, how to keep it and how to make it grow; here is what I tell them. "After you've re-defined success for yourself, written down your short term and long term goals with deadlines, created a goal board so you can keep your goals in plain sight, made the decision to consciously thing BIG, actively done something each day to pursue your passion and identified your WHY, then it's time to cut down on your current expenses and think of ways to make your future expenses controllable". To tackle the latter portion, start by creating a budget, which we discussed in the previous chapter. Analyze all of your monthly bills and ask yourself how can you cut back on each; so you'll have money to save in order to clear bad debt or invest in various forms of investments like paper assets, real estate, a business or creating streams of passive and residual income. In this chapter I'll be listing some ways that you can save on some of your biggest expenses.

After you've created your budget and listed ways where you can save on each expense then it's time to brainstorm ways on how you can bring in more money. Because it doesn't matter how much you're cutting back, if you don't have enough money coming in so you can start investing, then you still won't get ahead financially.

Once you have your budget established, have your expenses under control and have extra income coming in, then it's time to eliminate your debt so you can not only improve your credit, but also have piece of mind.

ELIMINATING DEBT

In order to get out of debt you first have to know how credit works. I think it's sad how many people get suckered into getting a credit card before they know how to efficiently manage debt; especially college students. Have you ever stopped to wonder why college students are the easiest among us to be approved for credit cards? What does someone coming straight out of high school know about budgeting or successfully managing debt? Chances are NOTHING! And that's exactly why they're the most targeted victims of credit card companies.

In addition to this chapter, I'd recommend that you read *"Credit Repair Kit for Dummies"* and *"The Complete Idiot's Guide to Improving Your Credit Score"*. Both are easy reads and pretty straight forward. Then you have to make a commitment to not take on any new debt period. No payment plans and no layaways (that incur interest), no Rent-A-Center, no payday loans, no title loans, no expensive phones that require a payment plan to pay it off, and no auto loans. If you can't afford to pay for it cash then simply don't get it. If this sounds easier said than done then look up a *free* debt program in your area. Not debt consolidation companies that charge you just to roll over all your debt in one single account, but a non-profit debt counseling service. One that I came across on the Internet is HOPE (Helping Ourselves to Prosper Economically), is a financial stability program offered by Housing and Credit Counseling Inc.

What open accounts do you have that you are currently making interest payments on? Analyze each account and close them if you don't absolutely need it. To get out of debt you have to make sacrifices. It may mean sending back the furniture you're making monthly or weekly payments on, and buying something used until you can save up enough money to buy what you really want without financing it. It may mean not eating out for a few months, or carrying your lunch to work each day instead of buying lunch. It's time to make drastic changes for a while; your future and peace of mind depends on it. So start thinking of ways you can cut costs on just about everything so you can apply the money that you've saved to pay down your debt.

Don't be tempted! There is a hotline that you can call to get your name and number removed from companies that call you about credit offers; call as soon as possible and get your name removed so you won't be tempted to sign up for any of their offers. To opt out for five years or permanently call toll-free 1-888-5-OPT-OUT   (1-888-567-8688)   or visit www.optoutprescreen.com.

UNDERSTANDING YOUR CREDIT SCORE

Credit scores range from 300-850.

Excellent
800-850 is the best credit score range there is. You are in the highest tier of potential borrowers and will get approved for anything you apply for.

Very Good Credit
There isn't much of a difference between 750 and 800. As long as you fall within that range you're going to get approved and offered the best rates.

Good Credit
700-749 is going to get you approved for the most part. You will be eligible for most loans, most insurance and most credit based jobs.

Fair
650-699 is an "acceptable" or "average" credit score. In this range creditors will start picking your credit apart to see exactly why your credit scores are what they are. If you do get approved expect higher fees, interest rates, and even insurance premiums.

Bad

600-649 is bad credit (also referred to as "subprime" credit). This may be a result of poor payment history, collection accounts, bankruptcy filings, or excessive credit card debt.

Very Bad

300-599 is the absolute lowest credit score range. At this point not even down payments or collateral is likely to help you get approved. It will even be hard to obtain insurance and any employers who check credit reports won't hire you.

After you've made that commitment to yourself then the next step is to monitor your credit. Get free copies of your credit report from www.annualcreditreport.com, or from each of the three credit bureaus by visiting www.Equifax.com, www.Experian.com and www.Transunion.com, (you're entitled to one free one a year from each). Keep in mind that only your credit *reports* are free; you'll have to pay to see your actual credit *scores*. If you have bad credit you may feel intimidated by all the negative and collection accounts, but in order to fix the problem you must first face the problem.

Your **payment history** counts for 35% of your credit score calculation; this category has the most effect on your score. Unfortunately missed and late payments are not easily fixed and often stay on your credit report for 7 years (even after you catch up on your payments or completely pay the account off). So if you have any accounts that you've fallen behind on, your first priority should be getting current. In order to avoid missed or late payments in the future, you should set up automatic bank drafts or multiple payment reminders so you can bills on time. Or maybe it will be easier for you to remember to pay them if you make it a habit of paying all your bills on one day.

The **amount of debt** you owe counts for 30% of your credit score calculation; this category has the second biggest effect on your score. So in order to get your score high and keep it there, keep your balance low on all your lines of credit. Try not to use more than 30% of any of your credit lines. If you don't have enough money at the moment to pay off all your accounts, set goal to pay off 70 % of each.

Credit history counts for 15% of your score. The longer your history, the higher your score will be. So when you finally pay off your accounts, don't completely close the accounts out if they are in good standing and you had them for a long time.

A **mix of accounts** and **new credit** both count for 10% of your score. So if you have a mix of installment credit, revolving credit, a mortgage, an auto loan and 3-5 credit cards (in good standing), your score will be at its highest.

Opening several credit accounts in a short period of time makes you seem like a greater risk to lenders, especially if you don't have a long history. So don't have your credit pulled unless you absolutely have to.

Also, whenever there is an inquiry or when most companies pull your credit your score goes down, unless it's a soft inquiry. A soft inquiry is an inquiry that occurs when a person or company pulls your credit report as a background check, like when you check your credit score or a mortgage lender preapproves you for a loan, or a utility company checks your credit to see if they'll require a deposit. So unless it's a soft inquiry, your credit score will drop a few points every time you apply for something...even if you aren't approved. So be very careful of companies giving you free items to see if you qualify for whatever they're trying to approve you for. Don't have your credit pulled unless you absolutely have to.

RAISING YOUR CREDIT SCORE

Monitor your credit reports. If you know you will be applying for something like a house soon, it would be wise to start monitoring your credit from a few months prior. All three credit bureaus have credit monitoring service where they'll alert you if there are any activities or inquiries on your account. Because the last thing you want to happen is something negative hitting your report and lowering your score right before you apply for a loan and not have a chance to correct it.

Make a list of all your debts. Make sure to list the name and phone number of creditors, interest rate, outstanding balance and minimum monthly payment. (Remember to include loans not listed on your credit reports like family loans and medical bills). Nothing gives you the courage to take on the future and peace of mind like knowing you don't owe anyone anything!

Start the dispute process. If there is anything negative on your report that is over seven years old, write a letter to each credit bureau asking them to remove it or use their online dispute form. In most cases after seven years they'll honor that request. Scan your credit report for discrepancies; even if your name is spelled wrong or it is showing that the amount you owe isn't correct, you can dispute it. The creditor has

30-45 days to respond, and if they don't in time then that debt is deleted. Information regarding lawsuits, liens, judgments, late child support, or other late payments should be deleted from your credit report after 7 years (and bankruptcies should be deleted after 10 years). So, in terms of your credit score, if your debt is that old or older, paying it will not help you. If the debt is approaching the 7 year mark, in some cases, paying the debt may even revive it on credit bureau reports and it may show up for another seven years, which could hurt you.

Negotiate with your creditors. Try and talk to your creditors before your account goes to collections because they have the power to remove late payments, late fees, interest fees, and other charges, if they really want to, so ask. Be positive, polite and most of all persistent. If the representative you are speaking to can't help you, don't hesitate to negotiate with a supervisor. If your account has already gone to collections then try and negotiate with the collectors, because even though late payments affect your credit reports and scores, collection accounts can result in even greater damage. Keep notes of the people you speak with at the collection agencies or credit bureaus, like their names, date and time you contacted them and the date by which any corrective action will be taken. (Always check your credit report again after that date to make sure they followed through. Corrections made on one credit report should automatically reflect on the other two as well).

Negotiate with your collectors. If it is in fact too late for you to negotiate with your creditors, then try and work something out with the collection agents. Try to negotiate fees to be waived and to see if you can pay less then the balance owed. Make sure that if they agree that you can pay less than the balance owed to settle the account, have them send you something in writing that says on your credit report it will show "paid in full". This is important because some lenders consider "settled for less than balance owed" to be a negative thing, and also because the remaining balance can be sold to another debt buyer who can still call you about it.

ESTABLISHING GOOD CREDIT

Start making payments. The *smartest* thing to do is to pay off the accounts that have the highest interest rates first because that will save you money in the long run. The *easiest* thing to do, however, is to pay off the accounts that have the smallest balances first. Because when you start seeing quick progress this will give you the push you need to keep tackling the next account, and then the next account. If you plan on making payments instead of one lump some payment, then mail them checks. Do NOT give them your debit card number because legally they can withdraw ALL the money you owe them from your bank account and you will not be able to do anything about it...because after all, you *do* owe them.

Paying off ANYTHING on your credit report that says, "charged off" will not help your score one bit. Charged off means that the original creditor has given up on being repaid according to the original terms of the loan and considers the remaining balance to be bad debt. So if you make any payments after that point it won't help your credit at all, because the ultimate damage has already been done.

Unless you plan on paying your debt immediately, it is important to remember that you can't contact the creditor or acknowledge the debt with the creditor. (Especially when they call you.) When you do this, the time clock of 7 years does start over from the most recent date of acknowledgement.

When you're ready to make a payment, you must not only pay off the debt in collections, but you must also negotiate to have it removed from the report all together (prior to you making the payment, and get it in writing). This will help you gain points, because just paying off the debt in collections alone will NOT improve your credit score.

Get current. Get up to date on late payments and missed payments as soon as you possibly can, because those two things hurt your credit score the most. Once you get current, stay current.

Check your current limits. If you recently got an increase on any of your credit limits make sure that it is reflecting on your report. If you haven't had a recent credit limit increase, then request that your limit be raised.

Get a credit card. (I just cringed as I wrote that). For years I've lectured to people to stay *away* from credit cards. But it's a sad fact that cash is no longer king...credit is! In fact, that's how most millionaires get their start, (they borrow money from banks in order to invest in their business ideas). But banks won't lend you money unless you can prove to them that you know *how* to handle money; and that's the purpose of a credit report. It is unfortunate that the balance in your savings account doesn't prove this to them, or how responsible you are using your *debit* card, or paying your monthly household bills on time doesn't prove this to them either; but it is what it is, so follow my advice and you'll stay on top. Get one or two lines of credit, because even "no credit" is like having bad credit.

Do your research, take your time and find out which cards works the best for you. Does a card with no annual fees appeal to you or does a card that maximizes your frequent flyer miles better fit your needs? When you do get a card, be strategic about it and get it from a company that you already do a lot of business. For instance, if you fly a lot you may want to get a card with an airline so you can reap flight benefits, or if you shop on Amazon a lot you may want to get a card with them. Or if you have a Bank of America account you may want to get one with them so you can get some of their rewards like 3% on cash back on gas (if you do a lot of driving). Having one or two lines of credit will definitely increase your score if you are responsible.

Get a "secured" credit card. If you don't feel like you are disciplined enough for credit cards, there is another option. You can get a "secured" loan or a "secured" credit card from your local bank or credit union. A "secured" account simply means that you will give the bank the same amount of money that you want to borrow, and they will hold on to it until you close that account.

Keep your balances low. To keep your score at its highest you should never go over 30% on any credit line. Ideally you should stay under 10%, (even if you usually pay of your whole balance monthly before it's due).

Piggyback! Get added to someone else's credit line as an "authorized user". Assure them that they don't even have to give you a card, and that you don't need to *use* their line of credit. You just need your name, date of birth and social security number added to their account in order for their payment history to show up on your credit report. It is EXTREMELY important that they have no late payments on that account in the past (or for as long as your name is attached to it), because your score will go down if they don't make their payments on time.

Don't close out any credit cards. Don't close out any cards that you've paid down to a zero balance (if they are in good standing and you've had for a long time because that will decrease the length of your account history. And don't totally stop using your current credit cards. Once you pay down the balance to zero making a small purchase of even $5 a month once a month will keep that card in good standing, (because if cards are inactive for long period of time then the issuer has the right to close that card down). Unfortunately, the whole way credit is accessed is based off of your usage. So if you don't use the lines of credit you have periodically, your score won't increase.

Protect your history. When you decide to cancel some of your credit cards, it's better to keep the old ones. By keeping your older cards open it shows more responsibility and consistency. Just remember that just having old cards isn't enough, you have to actively use them; so make at least one small purchase every few months and pay it off that same month.

INSURANCE

Basically, Insurance is a means of protection from financial loss. The insurance transaction involves the insured person making payments to the insurer in exchange for the insurer's promise to pay the insured in the event of a covered loss. It's very important that you tell the truth when answering all the questions in the application process. Because the last thing you want to do is get approved and then pay your monthly premiums for years, just to get denied when you file a claim.

I'm going to cover a few different types of insurance. Every type of insurance isn't ideal for everyone; one policy does not fit all. Analyze each to see which one is in your best interest.

LIFE INSURANCE: No one likes to think about it, but none of us will live forever. With that said I believe that all of us should have life insurance. Even if you don't have family to leave the money for, having a life insurance policy is a good idea if you don't have any money saved. Because at the very least it can be used for your own burial costs so that burden isn't left for someone else. The earlier you purchase life insurance the less it costs. Shop around for the best rates and see if the insurance company you select will give you a discount if you pay a year in advance or if you sign up to have your payments deducted automatically from your checking account monthly.

Life insurance helps protect your family financially when you die by helping cover the cost of lost income, funeral expenses, outstanding debt and education cost for children. It's great coverage to have. Your age, marital status, your dependents, your debt, your assets, and whether you'll have estate taxes should all play a factor when deciding if you should buy life insurance.

If you have a spouse, children or other people who rely on you, then it's best to have adequate insurance to cover all their needs after you are gone. Consider the quality of life you want your dependents to have after you're gone when deciding how much life insurance you should buy. For instance, will they need to replace your income, will you haven any outstanding debt like a mortgage for example, and do you want your kids to be able to afford college?

There are different types of life insurance. Some include: term life, permanent life, a combination of the two, and accidental death and dismemberment.

Term life is cheap because it has no cash value and it's temporary.   It's intended to provide lower-cost coverage during times when people may need it most, like when they're starting a family, paying off debt, paying off their mortgage or saving for college.

Whole life insurance payments are much higher than *term* insurance because there's a guaranteed rate of investment return, it covers you for a lifetime, and it has cash value, that you can withdraw from to use as collateral for a loan, or even use it to make future premium payments.

Accidental death insurance: Accidental pays out if you were to die from an accident. It may be offered to you as a rider on your regular life insurance policy or can also be purchased as its own policy. The likelihood of death from an accident is 1 in 20. To pay extra for this uncommon chance of death is not worth the more costly premium. It's better to get a lower cost term life insurance policy because it will pay out for all forms of death, whether from an accident, disease, or natural causes. Or use of your money to increase the coverage on your regular life insurance.

Speaking of life insurance, if you have assets, a business or any money, it's in your best interest to have a trust, estate plan and a will. Because if you die without those in place the government has the power to allocate those things the best way it sees fit. At the very least it may cost your loved ones dearly in probate costs.

HEALTH INSURANCE: is one of the best investments you can ever make, because if you get sick and you'll still need money to pay your rent and bills. Insurance can help you to make ends meet if you are unable to earn income because of health reasons.

Some types of health-related policies include:

Mortgage protection insurance: which pays your mortgage if you can't work.

Trauma insurance: which provides a lump sum if you suffer from certain illnesses or injuries.

Income protection insurance: which pays a portion of your income on an ongoing basis while you're sick.

Medical insurance: which covers hospital and other medical bills.

DISABILITY INSURANCE: Pays out a lump sum for permanent disablement through an accident or sickness. It helps cover your loss of income from some types of disabilities that cause you to lose your job, or prevent you from earning money. You're way more likely to be injured than killed, so it's probably smart to have some of this insurance. Most employers have a basic disability policy for their employees. But that might not be enough for you, or you may be self-employed. If you're self-employed should really look into this type of coverage.

HOME OWNERS INSURANCE: Is insurance on your home that protects it in case of fire or other damage. Before you get your house insurance you need to decide how much it would take to rebuild our home in the event of a disaster. In return for your insurance payments you get peace of mind, that if something were to lose your home, to a fire, earthquake, flood, storm, you would be repaid for the damage.

CONTENTS INSURANCE: is coverage for property or valuables you own. With this kind of personal property protection, you're covering the possessions that are in your home. It can be your computer, art collection, wine collection, jewelry, appliances or clothes. If you're renting a home and disaster strikes, your landlord will be covered for structural damages through *their* insurance, but you won't be covered if everything inside your rental is damaged. As a tenant, it's your responsibility to take out an insurance policy that will reimburse you for what you own if it were to suddenly be destroyed or stolen. If you have things that would be expensive to replace, this is definitely the kind of insurance you want to have.

TRAVEL INSURANCE: It's a good idea to buy travel insurance whenever you take an international trip. Travel insurance policies cover your personal items against loss or theft, extra costs accumulated if your flights are cancelled, and medical treatment if we have an emergency or get sick. Medical bills can be very costly in other countries so it can be a big financial risk to go on international vacations without travel insurance.

Travel insurance policies usually have exclusions for pre-existing conditions and luggage left unattended. There are many conditions and exclusions in travel insurance policies, so you have to read the fine print in each policy to see exactly what is covered.

AUTO INSURANCE: A car may be one of the most expensive items we own and can be very costly to replace if stolen or damaged in an accident. Auto insurance will pay to repair or replace your car if any of these things occur.

Though insuring your vehicle is mandatory, the level of coverage you choose is flexible. Monthly insurance rates will vary widely depending on your age, type of vehicle, claims history and the deductible you choose.

'Comprehensive' motor vehicle insurance is the most common and it covers us for loss, theft or damage to our vehicle. It also covers us for accidental damage to the other car or property we damage.

Cheaper options are 'third party' and 'third party, fire and theft' cover. Third party insurance covers for damage to another person's vehicle or property, but not yours. (Extending third party insurance to fire and theft covers the risk of our car being destroyed by fire or stolen, too).

*In this chapter I chose to cover **credit** and **insurance** because I believe that these are two vital pieces to getting ahead due to the way the system is designed. If you have good credit you can essentially get anything you want, and if you have the right kind of insurance then you can secure all that you accumulate.*

I'm so tired of self-help books telling me what I "should" do; That I need to "manage my time", "get organized", "automate my life", "prioritize", "be prepared", "protect my assets", but failing to point out actually ways that I can do all of those things. So I gave you all that and more in this book. I'm a firm believer in giving more than what's expected of me, so I hope this book lived up to my life's philosophy.

CLOSING

Why I wrote this book...

On July 29th 2012, a stray bullet shot my fifteen-year-old sister Danielle. She was riding in the back of our parent's minivan when a man on the street opened fire at someone else. A bullet came through the van, shattered the glass window and lodged in Danielle's head. It paralyzed her leaving her unable to walk or talk. It really shook me up. It made me analyze my life and ask myself, "If something like this were to happen to me what would I regret not doing and most of all...when I leave this world, how do I want to be remembered?" I came to the conclusion that I would have regretted not spending more time with my family, I would have regretted not seeing more of the world and I would have regretted not giving back more...so I worked on those things.

I started spending more quality time with my immediate family. I made a list of all the places in the world that I wanted to see and I started traveling to them and started giving back. I'm giving back by volunteering for "Susan G. Komen" breast cancer organization, feeding the homeless some Sundays in downtown Atlanta and I started my non-profit", The E.L.M. Society, (which stands for Entrepreneurship,

Literacy and Mentorship, because I feel like those are the most effective solutions to eliminate poverty).

What I'm most proud of is starting is "The Goal Group". Its main focus is to group individuals based on their goals. I found there was a great need for it because when people reached out to me for guidance they always felt like they were alone because no one in their immediate circle was supportive or had the same goals that they had. I was the one common link among all these people and it only seemed logical to connect them with each other. So whether people want to get fit, further their education, advance in their career, start their own business, meet other single parents, or just develop a social life I would pair them up with like minded individuals so they would have a support system. Within the company I conduct "Design Your Life" workshops, teaching people about goal setting, financial freedom, overcoming obstacles, & dating smarter.

Through Danielle's tragedy I found my purpose, which is to help other people find *their* purpose. I do so through my workshops, through my free YouTube tutorials, through my life coaching services and though my books...such as this one. I hope you enjoyed it because I truly poured all my heart and being into it. I packed it with lessons I learned through trail & error, through books & mentors, through traveling & taking risks. I trust that you not only READ it, but also APPLY the knowledge and GIFT a copy to a friend or two because your chances of succeeding doubles when you have someone on the success journey with you.

Ps. if there is something that I can assist you with...and you have a product or service you can offer in exchange...then don't hesitate to send me an email with "Let's Barter" in the subject line!

TURN THE PAGE...TO STAY IN THE LOOP!

STAY IN THE LOOP!

If you enjoyed this book, help me to reach other people by heading over to amazon or the site that you bought it from NOW and leave a review :)

Check out my other books:
A GOAL Digger's Guide (How to get what you want without giving it up) and The Break Up Guide (How to get over it in half the time) on Amazon and listen to them on Audible.com

If you're interested in one-on-one life coaching in person, over the phone, through video chat or through email, then email me at iLoveBaje.com

Follow me on Facebook @ MissBaje
And on Instagram @MissBaje @TheGoalGroup
@aGOALdiggersGuide @DesignYourLifeWorkshops

Linkedin.com/in/Missbaje   Periscope @MissBaje

Twitter @ModelBaje,   Snapchat @MissBaje1

Subscribe to Youtube.com/BajeFletcher for my free tutorials

Most Importantly, subscribe to www.TheGoalGroupinc.com and www.MissBaje.com for updates, giveaways, my documentary of my life, and to see when my DESIGN YOUR LIFE workshop will be in your city.

Made in the USA
Lexington, KY
08 June 2017